Dear Patty,
    I Am Extremely Delighted
We Met. — I Always
Enjoy Our Conversations.

    Remember, There Are No
Coincidences In Life Every
Thing Happens For A Reason.

    Best Of Health,

    Lee

    5/2/08

P. S.: Thank You For Being The
Person You Are — God Bless!

Left to Right: Tom Downing and George Brown up on unidentified horses.

A Forgotten Horseman:

A Son's Weekend Memoir

Lee E. Downing

ISBN: 1-59975-880-6

Dedicated To...

Thomas and Irene Downing
Your love and spirit will always be with me

To...
Iva Wess
I will always treasure the numerous phone conversations over the years
we had and the note you sent entitled, "Great Men With Great Horses".
Thank you for your inspiration.

To...
Claude "Beanie" Johnson
Thank you for sending the photos of Dad along with the horse
magazines during Dad's days as a horseman in Kentucky. You are the
greatest brother-in-law a man could have.

To...
Naomi and Amber—my donor's daughters
Your father's love lives within me. God Bless you, your mother Loretta
and your family for saving my life.

To...
The Forgotten Horsemen
I will never forget you and that special summer weekend and the
impact you had on my life. "Keep your heels down in those stirrups."

Acknowledgement

Tom "Slick" Wess, Jim Frye, Stanley Jackson, Sam "Grinney" Ransom, Carl Conner, Beauford Hall, Frank Gay, Kit Biddle, Tom Butler, George and Howard Brown, William and Eddie Stivers, Jim Martin, Bill Nelson, Ted Morris, Marion Russell and Thomas Downing are some of the names of the men I affectionately call *The Forgotten Horsemen*. Many are from the saddlehorse kingdom of Lexington, Kentucky or more precisely, North Middletown, Kentucky. They rode and trained American Saddlebred horses for wealthy white men throughout the country as their profession. Although they seldom received the recognition and respect for their craftsmanship, somehow they kept their sense of pride and dignity throughout the most difficult of times, while the rich and wealthy horse owners claimed the credit.

Their success, along with many trials and tribulations, was preceded by the success of the legendary Tom Bass, the first noted Black Horseman. Unlike my dad and the fellow horsemen of his era, Tom Bass became a legend, yet he too in the archives of history, remains largely unknown. In fact, to place history in perspective, before Jack Johnson won the heavyweight boxing title, before Jackie Robinson became a Dodger, before Rosa Parks refused to move to the back of the bus and before Martin Luther King led the Civil Rights movement, there was Tom Bass leading the way, breaking the color line and becoming a hailed horseman. It was Tom Bass who paved the way for my dad and the other Black horsemen who followed him in the world of the Saddlebred Horse training.

A special thank you to Bud Butler, Kim Skipton and Dick Kearny for sharing your resources and knowledge. You greatly helped refresh my memory.

Some of the names of individuals and names of horses have been changed in large part because of insufficient available information.

Forward

"What is essential is invisible to the eye."

- Antoine de Saint- Exupery

When I was sixteen, I held my dad's hands while on my knees pleading to God for him not to die. "Dad, dad, dad," I cried out, as he lay there on his back with his hands and fingers in a firm position grasping the reins of a five gait mare. He was in a place of contentment as he spoke, "Whoa mare, that's a girl!" and made those familiar clicking sounds that I often heard when I was a little boy watching him ride the horses everyday in the summer. Then in a calm moment, with his hands gently relaxed in mine, his face revealed a soft smile and he took his last breath and his last ride.

My father, Thomas Downing was a horse trainer, one of the forgotten horsemen who was born and raised in the Saddlebred kingdom of North Middletown, Kentucky. He had a natural, uncanny and remarkable gift of relating to horses, proven by the trust and confidence exhibited by the horses toward him. Although my dad was a man of few words, his true voice, a voice that spoke volumes, was spoken within his work and accomplishments with the horses he trained. He often preferred to spend time with the horses over most people and it was that bond which enabled him to train the horses so effectively.

This book is about a summer weekend I spent as a ten year old boy helping my father at a horse show and the invaluable lessons of life I learned from my dad and his fellow forgotten horsemen, who a contemporary of theirs called them, "Great Men with Great Horses". It was over this weekend I would learn more about my father, horses and life than I ever thought imaginable.

Prologue

1976

Kean College

Union Township, New Jersey

"Class, welcome to D-Day," I say with a sarcastic calmness that eases the thick and heavy tension in the room. "As you all know, today you will take your final exam. This test will account for 30% of your final course grade. Mr. Anderson, can you please come up here?"

Looking up and glancing across the small room before me, the faces of youth, eager to learn but visibly apprehensive about their final exam, look back in my direction.

From the front row, the young aid walks over and grabs a stack of tests from my grasp. As he then hands them out, I continue on, "This is a timed test. You will have forty-five minutes to complete it and you may want to start with the multiple choice section prior to the essay. I would hate to see any of you not be able to finish the exam because you are lost in trying to write the perfect composition."

The class of about twenty chuckle in response. Their reaction triggers a memory of a familiar experience within me. As a youth in primary school, I remember the test anxiety that so often plagued me. Something as simple as a pop quiz would send me into a spell of dizziness and shortness of breath. To make matters worse, times were different then. A young Black child had no place making a scene in a predominately-White classroom... or so it was silently 'understood'.

The anxiety affliction would have plagued me all my life if not for a summer spent with my dad where I learned more about competition and life's tests than I ever would have thought possible otherwise.

Smiling at the thought and wanting to usher out a similar comfort to the students in my class, I then add in, "Each of you knows every answer on this exam. Don't think about your grade... just take each question one at a time and you will do fine." All together, the class exhales a sigh of relief. As a junior professor in the Health and Recreation Department at Kean College, my colleagues and I always had a knack for communicating with younger, thirsty minds and it is because of that zest our department and classes were so popular.

With the tension lifted, I finally raise my hand with enthusiasm and say, "Begin!"

On my words, the students all lower their heads and begin the nervous scribbling of lead onto paper. With nearly an hour to spare, I turn back around toward the desk and descend into an old wooden, classroom professor's chair. Unsure of what to do to pass the time, my thoughts are soon seized by a soft and warm breeze sifting in from the slatted screen of the nearby window. Desiring to feel the light wind on me fully, I turn my head toward the window.

Upon doing so, my eyes catch sight of three horses in the distance, grazing on a green field adjacent to the classroom. The sight enamors my senses, seemingly willing my soul closer to the window for a better look. As if led by a guiding hand, I once again stand, but this time move toward the window. I slide the glass to the left, increasing the width of the opening. The slight scratch that accompanies the movement goes unnoticed to the class, much to my delight. With a sharp gaze and the warm wind now fully upon my face, I take a closer look at the three horses.

The sight of a horse, any horse, lights a spark within me. I like to think I know not why… to instead pawn it off as some unanswered truth about love and life. However, the reality is I know fully well that my adoration for the poised animals goes far beyond any appreciation of species. Rather it is the symbol of life and freedom associated with them that I love. You can start with their history and end with their gracefulness, but in between, where true respect is born, is the memory of a young boy and his father that fills my thoughts. It is hidden within that memory where I find my love for horses and to this day, that love has never diminished.

Over the years, I have had the opportunity to learn about horses and horse shows on various occasions. The American Saddle Horse, for instance, began in the 1600's when the foundations for the American Saddlebred were established. This happened when Galloway and Hobby horses were brought to North America by British colonists.

In the 1800's, American horses convoyed pioneers west into Kentucky. Then, in the war of 1812, Kentuckians mounted these horses to fight against the British and Native American allies.

After the war of 1812, the first recorded horse show was held in Lexington, Kentucky in 1817.

The American Saddle Horse gained fame as a breed during the Civil War. Saddlebreds served as the mounts of many famous generals; Lee rode 'Traveler', Grant on 'Cincinnati', Sherman rode 'Lexington', and Stonewall Jackson's mount was 'Little Sorrell'. The three aforementioned horses were all of the American type with Thoroughbred genes running through their blood, while the latter was of pacing stock.

After the war, this particular brand of horse flourished and because of the increased popularity and commercial value of the Saddlebred, enlightened breeders began to call for the formation of a breed association and registry. In response to the clamoring, Charles F. Mills of Springfield, Illinois, began compiling pedigrees and formulating rules for a registry. The Farmers Home Journal, a newspaper published at the time in Louisville, Kentucky, called for a meeting April 7, 1891 to organize the association. The registry was established that day... the first horse breed association in the United States.

From there, a coal black stallion named Rex McDonald burst onto the show scene at St. Louis in 1893 and made the largest single horse contribution ever, giving even greater status to shows and breeds. He was only beaten on three occasions and became the most famous champion saddle stallion that the world has ever known. He was idolized by the public and even visited by Presidents of the United States.

By this time, gifted horsemen began making a living by training show horses. Throughout the history of the trade, none has since been more talented than the incomparable Tom Bass, the first noted Black trainer and the original forgotten horseman.

A native of Missouri, in the early 1900's Tom Bass became one of the greatest American Saddlebred horse-trainers, entertaining the likes of President Theodore Roosevelt, Will Rogers, P.T. Barnum, Buffalo Bill Cody and many others.

The distinguished Tom Bass rode the invincible Rex McDonald and had a special bond with the horse.

At the time of his death, humorist Will Rogers wrote in eulogy of the first great Black horseman, "Tom Bass, well-known Negro horseman, age 75, died today. Don't mean much to you, does it? You have all seen society folks perform on a beautiful three or five gaited horse and said, 'My, what skill and patience they must have had to train that animal.' Well, all they did was ride them. All this Negro Tom Bass did was train them. He trained thousands that others were applauded on. A remarkable man, a remarkable character. If old St. Peter is as wise as we give him credit for Tom, he will let you go in on horseback and give those folks up there a great show and you'll get the blue ribbon yourself."

Over the centuries since, the love of the Saddlebred horses has only grown. American Saddlebreds have been successful in most equine disciplines from cow horses to jumpers, dressage to carriage horses. If conditioned and trained properly, Saddlebreds are capable of almost any task they are asked to perform... and they do it with style.

It is then, with the thoughts of the Saddlebred fleeting with the wind, when my mind shifts once more to another time, with my inner child leading the way and life's lessons laughing at the journey being used to get there.

In this memory, the warm breeze was the same and the sun shined just as bright in the late morning sky, but that was where the similarities ended. My eyes begin to swell as the floodgates of a time passed continue to fill my mind with the thoughts of another moment... another era.

When I was sixteen, I held my dad's hands while on my knees pleading to God for him not to die. "Dad, dad, dad," I cried out, as he lay there on his back with his hands and fingers in a firm position grasping the reins of a five gait mare. He was in a place of contentment as he spoke, "Whoa mare, that's a girl!" and made those familiar clicking sounds that I so often heard when I was a little boy watching him ride the horses everyday in the summer. Then in a calm moment, with his hands gently relaxed in mine, his face revealed a soft smile and he took his last breath and last ride.

The remembrance of my dad's death brings a tear to my eyes. Looking out from the classroom window though, I do not shut the emotion out. The memory of that time used to bring me to my knees, but over the years I have come to terms with the loss. Never forgetting my dad, I have come to realize his presence all around me and in everything I do. It was in that comfort where I found the strength to become the man I have.

After collecting myself, I look back at my students and see they are all lost in their own thoughts. Not wanting to waste the beautiful late morning, I pull the chair over to the window and relax. Only a few minutes have passed and the memories of my dad and the horses have ushered in a thought of another time. A time when a boy became a man. Taking advantage of the temporary freedom, I transfix my eyes on nature's painting before me and become lost in my own thoughts.

Chapter 1

Thursday, July 1959

Life is good. The intense orange sun is conveying a brilliance to the land, foreshadowing the warmth it will bring today. Its color fades restlessly into the wavy clouds in an attempt to push away the evening's darkness. Shortly, the sun will be resting fully overhead, raining its affection down upon us. I've always been fond of the heat. It feels as if nature is wrapping me in her arms with a home-fashioned quilt, one to rival the comfort of Momma's handiwork.

While kicking an old, worn-thin football around on the dried, dirt-packed ground with my PF Flyers, I notice my breathing is a bit labored. The nervousness alone has added sweat to my brow. However, it's not just the upcoming trip which is making me so anxious, but the fact that at this moment I still don't even know if I will be going. Dad's been promising me this outing for awhile now. I scored good marks in class and pulled extra duty around the house, but it looks as if he still needs to champion my cause.

Glancing over, I see my parents in a deep discussion, a debate that started last night and has not yet seemed to quit.

Momma loves me, but she worries too much. Since all her other children have grown up and gone, she now seems a little more over-protective of me, her last child. With my two sisters, Alice (nicknamed Tid), and Margaret (Pearl) married and living in North Middletown, Kentucky and Indianapolis, Indiana respectively, and with my oldest brothers Ralph and Henry married, living in Canton, Ohio and working for manufacturing companies, Momma's fears, worries and wisdom all focus on me. Harry, my closest brother in age, had it right in her eyes when he hit the books and went to college. She often tells me how that same life for me, one where education comes first, would make her proud.

While lost in that thought, my attention is broken as Mike, our light brown spotted Setter, stands up and pounces on the football I had been kicking around mindlessly. For the past few minutes he has been watching the battered pigskin and apparently decided now was a good time to overtake his 'prey'.

With my hands dug deep in my blue jean overall pockets and a smile on my face, I begin moving my body forward, closer to the house, with long strides. I am forced to cock my head slightly to the left and squint my eyes to keep out the ever-rising sun. Moving onward, I try to make as little noise as possible as I struggle to clarify the muffled sounds of my parent's conversation.

"I'm not so sure 'bout this Tom…" Momma says boisterously, never one to let her feelings go ignored.

"Listen," Dad replies softly. "I don't want him workin' horses all his life either. But if that's what he wants, I'm not gonna stop him. Makin' your own decisions is part of being a man. Besides, he's worked hard for this."

"But he's still my baby boy. He's never been away from the house this long before without me."

"He'll be fine Irene. Besides, he will learn more this weekend about life than he ever could from them books... and maybe the hard work will actually discourage him from pursuin' it. Also, we both promised him that if he made good grades and did his chores he could go. I ain't gonna go against my word now."

You tell her Dad, I whisper silently to myself as I hear my dad fight for me.

Knowing she is waging a losing battle leaves Momma speechless. It is then, from across the way, when a loud honk echoes into the air. Everyone's concentration breaks and we all watch as my Uncle JT pulls up in his 1951 Ford F-1. The beat-up old blue truck is his pride and joy, and never seems to let him down.

Though not my real uncle, Jim Thomas Martin (Uncle JT) has been a part of the family for as far back as I can remember. I had seen he and Dad work with the horses with a common efficiency for what seems like over a hundred times before. However, for all his skills and concentration, we also know that whenever Uncle JT is around, fun is never far behind.

Following close behind and coming up the winding road with the dust billowing is an enormously large, all white-colored horse trailer van. The entire vehicle is a bit worn down, but carries out its purpose well... the transport of our horses.

Running down the side are big and bold, black-decaled letters noting, 'Jim Frye Horse Trailer Transportation Incorporation of Ohio'.

Although the van was only twenty feet in length, it seems endlessly long as it slowly maneuvers up the slightly hilly road to the barn. The driver, Frank Stuart, Mr. Frank as I had come to know him, has on numerous occasions been hired by Dr. Bachtel, Dad's boss, to transport the horses to the various shows throughout the year. This weekend's show at the Canfield Fairgrounds is going to be my first opportunity to watch the horsemen first hand and knowing Mr. Frank was involved only meant the show was going to be a big event.

As Mike ditches the old ball and rushes toward the oncoming vehicles with a series of friendly barks, Dad bends over and kisses Momma on the cheek. In a huff, she turns and returns to the house while he motions me over with a wide, captivating smile.

Dad's cocoa brown skin, tanned even darker from the hours spent outdoors, glistens in the morning light. Atop his head rests one of my favorite hats, a brown and weathered bee-bop cap, tipped to the side, covering a thick-cropped bushel of all-white hair that makes him look even older than his fifty years. He walks tall and bow-legged, a typical byproduct of years spent atop horses. His stature is further accented by his wide, muscular shoulders which are often arched back, and his head which is always held high. I am both awed and proud whenever

I am around him.

As I reach him, he motions for me to stand by his side and rests his strong, steel-like hands upon my shoulder. Together we watch as the horse trailer arrives, causing the butterflies to dance in my stomach. After only a few minutes, both the F-1 and the horse van arrive at the barn and with an uninhibited excitement, Mr. Frank and Uncle JT approach us, ready for the long weekend ahead.

"H'lo Tom," Uncle JT says jubilantly with a Jamaican-English accent. Beside my Dad, JT is noticeably smaller in stature, but extremely muscular and strong. His midnight-brown skin complexion is accented by his clean-shaven head, as he was bald well before bald was popular. Then, glancing downward, his eyes meet mine and issue a nod of affirmation as if I was entering a secret society. "You ready boy?" he then adds as he grips my opposite shoulder.

"Yes sir! I'm ready!" I reply, my smile as big as those on the men who surround me.

Mr. Frank, a very thin ghostly looking white man in his mid-forties, then looks over at me and gives me the same nod of approval. Before he can say anything though, Dad's voice rings aloud in the air.

"A'ight people, lets get started. We have a long day ahead of us and I don't wanna start late," Dad interrupts, urging me over to the equipment he stacked earlier this morning.

Before me is what seems like a mountain of material. As I

look at the pile of equipment and tack, I am almost overwhelmed by the daunting task. But with everything I've been through to get in this position, there is no way I am going to start complaining now. Rope, brushes, saddlecloths, harnesses and more, are all prepped and ready to be loaded.

Looking at it, I then turn to Dad, "So, why do we load these first? Wouldn't it be easier to put the horses on first?" I ask this in attempt to try anything that will prolong the hard work that is piled in front of me.

Dad turns to me with a wry grin, looks down at the equipment and then back to me once more, "You gotta remember, what's easiest for us ain't always best for the horses."

"What do you mean?" I question as Uncle JT hands me a barrel of brushes.

"Irene always said this boy asks a lot of questions," Uncle JT interjects while giving me a nudge.

"Well... how long do you think it will take to load the trailer?" Just like Dad to answer a question with another question. He says it teaches me to think for myself.

Looking back at the equipment, I shrug my shoulders a bit before replying, "I'd guess about a half hour, give or take."

"And to unload it once we get there?"

"Another half hour I suppose."

Then with an added smile lacing his lips as he hands me a cord of rope, he next asks, "So how would you like to stand for an extra hour in a long, hot trailer, just because it was easier for me... Would you perform at your best?"

Just then, a loud roar rumbles out from both Uncle JT and Mr. Frank, and as I turn I see them shaking their heads in laughter.

Dad then picks me up and sits me atop one of our traveling footlockers. With our eyes on an even plain to each other he says to me, "Always remember Lee, the most difficult things to do are always the right things to do."

With an obviously puzzled look on my face, Dad then continues, "What I mean is the most difficult task in life that will challenge you will also happen to be the best thing for you. You might not know it at the time, because we generally don't, but in the long run you'll see that hard work and facing adversity head-on will always make you a stronger and better person."

Dad then places his hand behind my neck and adds, "Son, there ain't no shortcuts in life. 'Least not for us. So remember, the things in life that are difficult and never easy to achieve are always the best things for you. And it just so happens that for us right now, it also happens to be the best thing for these horses. You got that?"

"I think so," I answer, still with some reservation.

"Good thing... If you remember this, it'll help you later in life."

For the next hour, we work beneath the rising midmorning sun, loading first the equipment and then carefully the six horses behind it. At this competition, our stable house is entering three categories; the three and five gaits, and the fine harness. This time of year, Dr. Bachtel works my Dad maniacally, as they are competing almost every week. The summer months hold more competitions than any other time of the year and so they travel all over Pennsylvania, Kentucky and Ohio, hitting every event they can.

Upon completion of our immediate tasks, Dad then turns and asks, "You tired yet son?"

"No sir, not yet," I answer with a shake.

"Good. We have a lot of work ahead of us. Now let's go say bye to your Momma." Turning back, he then shouts, "Country Boy", a name he affectionately calls Uncle JT occasionally.

"Don't worry. I got it Mojo," Uncle JT replies to Dad with a familiar nickname of his own, "We'll be ready to go."

With that, Dad and I walk over to the house that sits only thirty yards away from the barn.

Resting on top a hill and noticeable for miles, both the house and barn are wooden structures originally painted white, but their original luster has faded due to time and the elements. For acres our home is surrounded by hay fields, which serve a dual purpose. The expansive land is great for training horses and the abundance of hay is fantastic for their sustenance.

Home… it is simple and quaint to say the least. Our six hundred square foot ranch style house has a kitchen, two small bedrooms, living room and one small bathroom in the basement.

Next to the house is an old water well, connected to a long, red metal handle that activates the pump. The house isn't much, but then again, I wouldn't change a thing.

Approaching Momma, I see a bag in her arms. Handing it to me, she then says, "Be good and be careful!" Then turning to Dad she adds, "And you Tom. You take good care of him."

"Yes honey," he replies, leaving a soft and gentle kiss on her lips.

Momma then kneels down and gives me a big hug, and as I look in her eyes I can see the tears welling up in them. Turning around to follow Dad to the horse trailer, I make sure to wipe the tears out of my own wet eyes. The truth is Momma is right. I have never been away from home for a weekend, and I am a little nervous. However, the time has finally come and the opportunity to spend time with Dad, in his world, was too good to pass up. Realizing as such, I walk toward the horse van without a second look back.

We head back to the trailer and walk up the van's ramp where the horses are. Dad cuts open a bail of hay and scatters it around in the middle of the van, adjacent to the horses in their traveling stalls. He next pulls out a blanket and pillow, and lays them down over the hay. Then looking at me he says, "Don't be afraid..."

I respond back with only pure, silent excitement as I crawl in under the blanket. *No way am I afraid,* I think as I try to truly convince myself of that very thought. I then watch as Dad goes over to one of the horses, King Cloud, and whispers into his ear in an almost inaudible tone, "Take care of my boy."

The horse responds with a snort, as if in acknowledgement. Dad pats King Cloud's thick brown mane in thanks, and then with a wink, he and Mr. Frank close the horse trailer door.

Within moments we are off, and as I listen to the sounds of the van's motor and feel our slow movement down the windy road it finally hits me. *We are on our way.*

Chapter 2

We have been traveling for over an hour and I have spent much of the time talking with the horses. Soon after pulling off our property, I stacked two bails of hay, one on top of the other, to give me the necessary height to watch from the small square ventilation windows of the van. I wanted to have the same vantage point as the horses when looking at the passing world. As I peer out with eager eyes and baited anticipation, I find myself jabbering away with King Cloud and the others.

It is only a two-hour drive to the Canfield Fairgrounds, but on this particular day Mr. Frank and Dad decide to stop off at the station outside of Bradley on the corner of Fifth and Washington. Years later, when recollecting the events of the weekend, I sometimes wondered why we did such a thing. Eventually, I began to understand. The world is not always fair, and in the eyes of a ten year old kid, that can be at times a difficult lesson to learn. Sometimes, unspoken education speaks the loudest words.

The Red Crown station is one of the newest and cleanest in the county. Dark red brick accents a sloped roof; it stands out amongst the dusty land. Two pumps rest in the front, with an attendant at each. The two white men wearing pressed, dark pants and clean white shirts with rolled up sleeves look ready to help. Atop their clean shaven faces rest black caps adorned with the Red Crown logo.

Excitement rises within me as I long to see them in action. From a distance, they issue us out a sociable wave and smile as the van approaches. Upon seeing that, I am instantly proud of the respect and recognition we garner as horse trainers, and from the small slit I am watching from I extend my hand out to reciprocate their welcoming gesture.

As I watch our approach from the side window of the van, Mr. Frank navigates the trailer up toward the pump. I am a bit surprised though when we do not stop there, but instead, continue on. Gazing out, my wide eyes catch sight of one of the attendants motioning us around toward the back of the building, and at the moment I did not fully understand why.

Within a minute or so, the trailer comes to a stop, captioned by the sound of hissing air releasing from the brakes. I wait patiently as Mr. Frank and Dad jump out of the horse trailer, closing the doors behind them with a soft slam. Without wasting any time, Dad and Mr. Frank come around the back, unhitch the latched lock, and open the large trailer door.

Bright sun instantly dilates my pupils, forcing my hand up to block out the brilliant rays. I hop out of the trailer just in time to see Uncle JT pulling his F-1 parallel to us. He jumps out joyously and I watch silently as my Dad and his two close friends interact, talking about the coming weekend.

I then turn around and peer around the corner out to the front of the station. I watch as the two attendants sit in folding chairs beside each of the clean pumps, kicked back and relaxed.

Just then, the baritone voice of Dad rings out into the air, "Son, you thirsty? Do ya want a pop?"

I shift back around and run over to the machine plugged in behind the building. I find cool refuge beneath the awning covering the soda-spitting appliance. The cola machine stands about a foot taller than me and is a deep red in color with a white wave at the top. It resonates softly with a quiet hum, as if urging us to it with a hypnotic mantra.

Dad drops in a dime for my pop, and a few more for him and the boys. For a moment, I loose myself in the cold liquid. Its refreshing taste helps battle the heat from the inside out. My happiness is soon broken though as Dad grabs my shoulder and says aloud, "You get to fill us up son."

In partial shock, I turn and motion to the attendants in the front of the building, "Aren't they supposed to do that?"

For a moment, Dad seems unsure what I am talking about, looking in my direction with an almost blank stare on his face. Suddenly it hits him and his smile quickly fades a bit. Not one to ever mince words, Dad replies with a calm and sensitive tone bearing no ill-will, "Those boys are only here to help the white folk."

I turn to him with a bit of disbelief. *We are horsemen... men... just like them*, I think to myself. The notion of the reality enveloping the events catches me somewhat by surprise. Our neighborhood around the farm in North Canton, Ohio was predominately white and even given that, although I had experienced prejudice before, I was never really witness to such institutionalized racism. However, for Dad and Uncle JT the occurrence out here in the 'real world' seems to be second nature… almost expected.

Before I could put any more thought into the subject, Dad speaks again, calming me with a tone familiar to that he uses with the horses, "Its ok. Don't think nothin' 'bout it. Any man that can't pump his own gas ain't a real man anyway."

His large grin and half-sarcastic tone brings a viral smile to my face, and soon all of us are laughing at a societal joke with no real punch line. Dad always had a way with lightening a tough situation, making the very best of it, and at this moment that particular gift came in handy.

Without another thought to the delicate situation, I run over quickly to the pump. The worn, metallic spout is obviously a left over artifact from a previous station and does not seem to fit in with the rest of the station which is clean and new. However, with a bit of finesse it works just fine. Devoid of any hesitation, I grip my fingers around the lever, forcing the pungent gas into the trailer's tank and for the next ten minutes enjoy my pop while listening to the conversation Dad, Mr. Frank and Uncle JT are engaged in.

The three men are standing away from the pumps, each enjoying a cigarette as they so often do. The pace of their conversation is quick and energetic, making it both easy and interesting to listen in on.

"So ya think King Cloud will place well this time 'round?" Mr. Frank says out, focusing the conversation.

"I think he has a real shot. The rack seems to be much easier for him. It's the toning down for the slow gait that'll be the problem," Dad responds as if he has thought it through a hundred times before.

"The five gait is the big show!" Mr. Frank exclaims.

"Yeah," Dad replies, "and Dr. Bachtel has made it quite clear he wants to do well in the big events. King Cloud is our best chance at that without a doubt."

"Hell," Uncle JT interjects, "If 'ole Tom here would actually ride in the show, there ain't nothin' that horse wouldn't do for him."

Blushing at the praise, Dad replies, "JT, you know I don't ride these horses in the show."

"Maybe so, but Pretty Boy does it... why don't you?"

"I told ya, it just ain't right for me. I've got my reasons as I'm sure some of the other trainers do too. Besides, Dr. Bachtel is a fine enough handler... he knows his horses well enough and he has a connection with 'em."

"Connection my ass," Uncle JT says back. "To him they ain't nuttin' but a weekend gloat around the clubhouse. And if

he's as calm and gentle with the ladies as he is with the horses…
it's a damn good thing he's rich."

The men all clamor out in laughter and I follow suit, unsure
of what exactly was meant by the comment but wanting to fit in
with these men I so adamantly respect.

Changing the friendly conversation Mr. Frank then adds,
"Speakin' of the ladies, how are things with you and Kat?"

Uncle JT's tone instantly calms and a soft light begins to
radiate from within his core.

"Look who's blushing now," Dad laughs out exuberantly,
nudging Uncle JT in the ribs.

It has long been known around our household that Uncle JT
has always held a place in his heart for Aunt Catherine (Kat), my
mom's sister. His love for her goes far beyond her good
cooking, which just so happens to be fabled by everyone.

"She's a tough nut to crack," Uncle JT replies with a boyish
grin I could even easily recognize.

" Don't worry JT, it'll happen," Dad says after finishing
his final gulp from the glass bottle. Then throwing it away in a
nearby bin he adds, "Besides, Irene is always tellin' me how
Kat's talkin' 'bout you. You just need to go on and talk to her."

"That's easier said than done," Uncle JT mumbles out as
Dad claps his hands loudly.

"Alright men, let's load up. We ready to go son?" Dad looks
at me and asks.

"Yes sir," I reply loudly.

"Good... we still have a long way to go and I wanna get these horses off the van and stalled up before lunch."

On those words, I toss my empty bottle into the same bin and follow Dad into the store to pay for the gas while Mr. Frank and Uncle JT return to their vehicles.

Inside the shop, Dad's deportment becomes calm and polite. On my best behavior, I follow suit.

"H'lo Tom," a short and portly black man says out from the aisle. "You got a show this weekend?"

"Sure do. Over at Canfield."

"Good luck." Then looking at me the man asks as he continues to restock the shelves, "Who's the lil' one?"

"He's my boy," Dad replies proudly. "He's helping me out this weekend."

"I hope you're good luck son... do your Daddy proud."

"Yes sir," I reply in a shy tone, huddled close to my dad's back. With a large grin on my face, I follow Dad up to a side counter. Once there, we are helped by a white man who is about the size of a bear. The short transaction is uneventful, but my dad's demeanor is obviously more controlled and sterile than it was just outside only a few minutes earlier.

On our way out the door, I give a look back to the stockman inside and he nods at me with a broad smile. I wave back a goodbye as I skip a short step in attempt to catch up with Dad who is now back at the trailer.

"C'mon boy," he says, ushering me back into the waiting horse van.

Picking up the pace, I run over and hop back into the trailer. Without a word, Dad, along with Mr. Frank, closes and latches the heavy door behind me and then they both quickly slide back into their seats in the cab.

Within a minute, I watch from my same perch within the van as Uncle JT's F-1 pulls back out onto the road. Quickly, Mr. Frank starts up the engine on the trailer and pulls out behind Uncle JT. As we hit the open road, I take a final look back at the station and at the two white attendants still sitting in their chairs, resting calmly beneath the shaded awning of the main pump island. And as we pull away, my mind contemplates what just happened.

Chapter 3

As we approach the famed Canfield Fairgrounds, my excitement is heightened as I suspect is the case for Dad, Mr. Frank and Uncle JT as well. While looking out through another small ventilation window that protects both me from the world and the world from my unabated exhilaration, I recall the history Dad shared with me about these long storied fairgrounds.

The Mahoning County Agricultural and Horticultural Society, founded at Canfield, Ohio, back in 1846, established the grounds to bring together the people and their products in the area to compare notes and relate experiences in a fair-like experience. The first fair was held on the village green, or commons as it was called then, and included a small livestock show, a plowing contest and a horserace or two. Early fairs were attended primarily by gentlemen, who dressed for the occasion in suits and top hats or fedoras.

Over the years, horse competitions such as the one we were to be a part of this particular weekend became common on the fairgrounds. The competitions are usually funded by old money and winning events brings with it a lasting prestige for both the owners and the men who train the winning horses.

Those thoughts are all fleeting from my mind as we make a left off Highway 20 and onto Ault Field Road. The level of excitement intensifies and even the horses seem to recognize the familiar territory, as they all begin to snort in accord.

Looking out over the horizon there are over one hundred vehicles in a parking lot off to the side of fairgrounds. Those vehicles represent the enormity of the event, as the area is already filled with workers, trainers, owners and the like.

Mr. Frank continues down the road, passing by the main fairground entrance. I bounce over to the other side of the trailer so I can view the scene. The tall, arched gate catches my eye and brings with it a sense of rising anticipation as I mouth the words of the large, ornate letters reading, *Welcome to the Canfield County Fairgrounds, since 1846.*

Over the years, this place was talked about endlessly by Dad and the other horsemen, and for the first time I am to share the unforgettable, fraternal experience with them.

Soon after we pass the main entrance, Mr. Frank navigates sharply off the main road and down a dirt path that leads to the back of the fairgrounds. I have to grip on tight to the base of a small window, as I do not want to miss a moment of the scenery.

We must have only been going about thirty miles per hour, but it seems to take us ten minutes to reach the back area. As we drive up, a man approaches the cab of the van. The words exchanged between him, Dad, and Mr. Frank are indistinguishable, but after a short conversation he waves us onto the expansive fairgrounds.

Once inside, Mr. Frank drives about one hundred yards along the left side of the interior wall and parks in front of a large stable. When we stop, the horses all let out impatient neighs, sensing the familiarity of the fairgrounds.

The murmurs and activity of the crowd are muffled from my position inside the back of the trailer. Just as the trailer door swings open though, my senses are ravaged by the various sights and sounds. The smell of roasted coffee hangs heavy in the air and the chattering, indistinguishable voices of mixed conversation ring in my ears. Wanting to see more, I deftly jump out of the back of the trailer.

My feet land hard against the dirt-packed ground. I quickly scan the entire area, ready for the challenge that awaits us. The view is even more intimidating from outside the horse van.

The wind is light and stale, but the very particular scent of horses fills the air. The sun is shinning as bright as it has all day. My head is spinning as the sights and sounds of the bustling activity around me cloud my already overrun senses.

"Get over here son," Dad calls out to me, interrupting my thoughts while handing me the reins of one of the horses, King Cloud. On reflex alone, I grab the smooth leather softly, my hands trembling.

"Are you o.k.?" he asks.

"Yeah, I'm o.k."

"Are you sure? You're looking a little pale there," Uncle JT interjects as he motions me to lead the horse down the steel ramp and out of the trailer.

"I'm sure he's just a bit nervous," Mr. Frank then adds in, coming to my aid. "Y'all remember the first time you came to an event like this. Hell, it still gets my blood pumping."

"True," Uncle JT replies while Dad looks with affirmation. Years later Dad explained, at that particular moment a wave of pride caught him. He realized then, if only to be for a weekend, horses were in my blood too and for a moment we understood each other.

Over the next few minutes we navigate out each of the six horses: King Cloud, a caramel chestnut brown stallion with four white socks and a white blaze who is a majestic beauty and the cornerstone of our equine fleet; Dell-ite, a smoky black mare with a gray blaze and flaxen mane and tail; Next To My Heart, a cocoa brown filly with two back white socks; Painted Doll, a chestnut brown mare with a light brown mane and tail; Ambassador, a dark chocolate brown stud with a brown mane and tail; and Hot Toddy, a midnight black stallion with white boots.

Unsure of where I am supposed to go, King Cloud seems to lead me. Holding on tight, we walk together to the stable. The entire structure is about twenty times the size of our house on the farm and there are numerous buildings in the area just like it.

Light brown, wood pillars hold up a slatted wood awning, which blends the barn into the single story series of adjoining stables. In all, there are about thirty open stalls all covered with various sets of brilliantly colored drapes representing the farms they are linked to.

The tack and stables that surround the horses are spectacular showcases, presenting the horses, the stables and the trainers who work them. The tacks of brilliant shining colors made of cotton and silk are the pride and joy of each stable. Just as a professional football team in uniformed colors, each individual tack displays the stable's name, bridged atop the rows of horses.

Our stable owned by Dr. David Bachtel, is called The Dells. Our logo is circular in nature, crafted of burgundy and gold with our stable name everywhere you could imagine, including the footlockers of the equipment, horse blankets, chairs, etc. Our tack is similar in craftsmanship to everyone else's, as thick as house drapes and forged of heavy cotton and silk that engulf the stalls in our stable, six for the horses and one which is our sleeping quarters. These drapes provide security for the horses, while also forming a customized, personal theater stage that forms a makeshift presentation area surrounding our equipment.

Our centering piece though, is the most fantastic of all. The header, as it is called, has a burgundy base, which is trimmed in gold with lettering saying, *The Dells* on top, and beneath that, *Owned by Dr. and Mrs. D.H. Bachtel of North Canton, Ohio.* Beside each header hangs the large ribbons of the stable's previous victories. These banners, drapes and awards help bring forth a sense of pride for everyone and the colors which craft them are something every stable house is proud of and protective over.

The term tack also encompasses any of the various accessories worn by horses in the course of their use as domesticated animals. For instance, saddles, stirrups, bridles, halters, reins, bits, harnesses, martingales and breastplates are all forms of specialized horse tack.

The saddles fasten to the horse's back by means of a girth or cinch, a wide strap that goes around the horse at a point about four inches behind the forelegs. Some saddles also have a second strap known as a flank cinch that fastens at the rear of the saddle and goes around the widest part of the horse's belly. It is going to be my job over the course of the weekend to make sure each saddle has to it a dazzling luster, looking its best for the competition. Presentation is as much a part of the show as skill.

It is important that the saddle be comfortable for both the rider and the horse, because an improperly fitting saddle may rub and cause the horse pain and eventual injury. Often times out of competition, but always in competition, a saddlecloth will be used that rests between the horse and the saddle, acting as a protective coating. Our saddlecloths all have the deep burgundy color, stitched with the gold circle designating Dr. Bachtel's stable, 'The Dells'.

Usually hanging next to the saddles, pegged into the walls, are the stirrups. Stirrups are supports for the rider's feet that hang down on either side of the saddle. Though underrated by most, the importance of stirrups is never ignored in Dad's eyes. He once told me how the invention of stirrups was of great significance in mounted combat, giving the rider a secure footing while on horseback. At the same time, the stirrups were also problematic due to the tendency for feet to get stuck in them in dire moments, causing the rider to be dragged. Because of this danger, tack manufacturers had since developed safety stirrups, which are either shaped to allow the rider's foot to slip out easily or are closed with a rubber band, and safety stirrup bars that are hangers for the stirrup leather that allow it to detach from the saddle in an emergency. For the purpose of our competitions, the standard invention is used.

Fleshing out the tack are the bridles and halters, which are an arrangement of straps around the horse's head used for communicating with the animal. Bridles contain a bit attached to the reins and are used for riding and driving horses. On the other hand, halters have no bit, are more general-purpose and most often equipped for leading or tethering a horse with one rein.

Double bridles, like a Bradoon or a Weymouth, use two bits in the mouth at once. The two bits allow the rider to have very precise control of the horse and usually only very advanced horses and riders use double bridles. Double bridles are typically seen in the top levels of show competition, as a horse's temperament is judged upon equally to that of style and grace.

The reins for the horses consist of leather straps attached to the outer ends of the bit and extend to the rider's hands. Reins are the means by which a horse rider communicates directional commands to the horse's head. Pulling on the reins can be used to steer or stop the horse. The sides of a horse's mouth are sensitive, so pulling on the reins pulls the bit, which then pulls the horse's head from side to side, which is how the horse is controlled.

A bit is a piece of metal that is placed in the horse's mouth, although on occasion the bit may be made of other materials. Despite the opinion of most, the bit does not rest on the teeth of the horse. Instead, it hangs in a space behind the front 'cutting' teeth and in front of the back 'grinding' teeth. This space is known as the 'bar'. When a horse is said to 'grab the bit in its teeth' they actually mean that the horse hardens its lips and mouth against the bit to ignore the rider's commands. Bits offer varying degrees of control and communication between rider and horse depending upon their design and on the skill of the rider. However, a good horseman can communicate just as effectively with a series of vocal ticks and soft strokes without relying on over handed control of the bit.

Each accessory for the horses has to be cleaned and polished, another chore of mine while here. Dad spoke endlessly in preparation of the trip, telling me the importance of such a job.

Although it would seem boring and tedious, he also told me how for the horse to perform his best, everything needs to be perfect. As such, every job, even that of the greenest stable boy was of equal importance and a victory for the horse would be a shared victory for all. That idea swelled a tide of excitement, and as I stared at all the tack, I understood what he meant.

After leading King Cloud into his stable quarters, I fastened the lock on the half-door behind him and headed back out to the van. Coming near, I see Dad surrounded by a group of men who are all are laughing and cajoling with friendly undertones.

To me, these men are larger than life. Sure, I am a fan of Popeye and The Lone Ranger, but these men before me are true stars. I have spent my entire childhood listening to Dad talk of them, seeing their pictures and imagining their company. I am speechless and held in awe by their presence.

This group of Bourbon County Horsemen, as they are mentioned, are Black horsemen who come from and mastered their trade in or around North Middletown, Kentucky. In fact, within a three-mile radius came the greatest group of Saddlebred horse farms in the country. The well-known stables of J.W. and Stoddard Young, A.G. Jones and Son, George Deatley, E.K. Thomas, Collins-Redmon, Biederman and Deatley, Robert Jones and H.S. Caywood and Son is where these men crafted their skills as horsemen. Collectively, they could have gone by any name and in my thoughts, I always imagined them to be the best horsemen around... "*The Mighty Middletown Horsemen.*"

Standing before me, Tom 'Slick' Wess, Stanley Jackson, Tom Brown, Beauford Hall, Tom Butler, Sam 'Grinney' Ransom, Frank Gay, Ted Morris, and Marion Russell are all at our tack, meeting and greeting each other as if at a family reunion. In addition to these men, Dad and Uncle JT, there is Uncle Bill Nelson, who like Uncle JT is not a blood relative. Bill Nelson stands over six feet tall, is very thin and lanky and has a coffee cream complexion emphasized by wavy, light brown hair and green eyes. He often spoke of being a child of interracial parents, which at the time and especially in his youth, must have been even a more difficult path to travel than being either all Black or all White. Uncle Bill is one of my favorite horsemen because he always makes the time to talk and play with me. This weekend however, I want things to be a little different. I am not here as a child, but rather, as a helper for Dad.

Also among the group is Pete Jones. With a light brown complexion, this handsome man was often called Pretty Boy. Standing about 5'10" tall, he is a dapper dresser and loves to show it off. He also is the only one of these Black horsemen who actually shows the horses for his owner of the stable. Because of that, many times Dad was urged to do the same for Dr. Bachtel. Nevertheless, even after watching Pete Jones ride, Dad still hesitated. He always felt more comfortable behind the scenes and never wavered from that thought.

Another of the horsemen in the group is Howard Brown, who also goes by the nickname Bulgia. I had heard stories of him in the past related by Dad, but this was the first time I ever recall meeting him in person. Bulgia and his brother George 'Dan' Brown, along with the twin Stivers brothers, Eddie and William 'Pigtail' are four other horsemen from North Middletown, Kentucky here for this weekend show.

As I stand watching these men, Uncle JT hollers over to me, needing help with the rest of the horses. I run over and help lead the remaining horses to their stalls. In the middle of my work, I catch sight of Dad looking at me and though he does not offer to help, I can tell he wants to. However, we both know that he can not seem over-protective and that I would have to prove to all these men that I could hold my own weight.

As they are talking, it is easy to notice the conversation change whenever Pete Jones, as boisterous as he is, would speak. Each man is boasting about their stable and their lead horse. Although these men are close as brothers, when it comes down to the competition, everyone wants to win. Friendliness remains, but the competitive fire for victory burns strong within each of them, a fire I often saw within Dad.

After each of the horses is stalled up, I am joined in the stable by Dad and Uncle JT. For a moment, the three of us stand in silence as we soak in the atmosphere. It is at that moment that I understood why Dad does what he does, and I realize the enormity of the work before us. We are here to win and not just for the sake of winning, but for the realization that comes with a certain amount of pride winning brings.

Once our moment of pause ends, Dad turns to me and says, "I need you to water the horses son. It's been a long day so far for 'em. Think you can handle that?"

While we have been able to refresh ourselves, the horses have traveled the duration of the trip with little respite. Traveling with them in the back of the van, I know firsthand of its confining heat, even with the small ventilation windows running across each side of the trailer.

"Yes sir, not a problem," I say as I grab a couple of large metal buckets while Dad gives me instructions as to the location of the spigot from which the main water line for the horses is supplied for the entire fairgrounds.

Without waiting a moment, I run over and place one of the buckets on the ground. With the other still in hand, I overlap the metal handle on top of the spigot, which is a bit hot to the touch after sitting in the sun uncovered all morning. Nimbly, I turn the handle and after a few seconds I hear the oncoming of water and begin to watch it flow into the hanging bucket.

After filling the two buckets, I grab one by the handle with each hand and attempt to carry the water to the horses about fifteen yards away. As I look down at the heavy pails, I struggle with each small step. Every motion rocks the buckets and the more I seem to concentrate on it, the more the water spills upon the ground.

While watching over from the stables as he is grooming one of the horses, Dad sees the trouble I am having. Considering this, he walks over to me and says with a soft confidence, "If you don't look at the water when you walk… it won't spill."

Upon hearing his words, I stop and put the buckets down with a mysterious disbelief. "How can this be true?" I ask, truly wanting to know the secret.

My parents always said I was like my sisters and brothers… always asking questions. As children, we were very inquisitive, a trait supported by my parents. It could not have been easy for them constantly fielding questions from us about anything and everything. However, they always wanted us to question the world and use every opportunity we could to learn new things. Because of that, neither Mom nor Dad ever became frustrated with our questions. At least it appeared that way to me.

Looking at me, he then replies, "Life has many mysteries. You'll see for yourself. Go ahead, try it. Just concentrate on completing your task and not the water you're carrying."

In response, I very slowly pick up the buckets again, look straight ahead and take a few steps. After closing the remaining fifteen yards, I reach the first horse, Hot Toddy and he snorts in appreciation of my approach. I gently set the buckets down and then quickly spin around.

My eyes trail along the path I just took and I see the ground is still and dry as a desert. I look up and see Dad smiling. To this day, I do not understand the 'why' behind the lesson, but it worked. And now, whenever I must complete any task I simply work toward the end, keep my faith along the way and remember

Dad's words about the most difficult things in life are often also the right things in life.

Chapter 4

For the entire day, Dad and the rest of the horsemen work diligently to prepare their stable tack and horses. All of the temporary stalls for each horse require fresh feed and fresh straw bedding to ensure the animals' comfort over the long weekend. In addition, to help keep them calm and rested, each horse is pampered with a therapeutic brushing.

The Thursdays leading into a competition are always of paramount importance. The goal is to calm and soothe the horses in such a way that they will be at their best for the weekend to come. In this time, they are treated as royalty, because upon their steady hooves rest the hopes of victory for every stable house.

The heat ravaged the fairgrounds today, but during the brutal hours just after noon, we had a small reprise from the sun in the guise of a passing rainstorm. The warm drizzling rain was just enough to make the entire day bearable and it cooled off the dry heat.

By this time, with dusk approaching, I find myself taking a small break from assisting with the brushing of the horses and unloading the essential accessory equipment from the footlockers and polishing them. Trying to gain a small reprieve from the day's labor, I sit on an old cardboard, Rolling Rock beer case. I am a bit hidden, leaning against the backside of the stable, sipping on a pop and reveling in our accomplishments.

My break lasts only ten quick minutes or so, but it is enough time to regain the strength within me and enjoy the moment. We just finished watering, feeding and brushing all the horses, and all the tack has been organized, polished and is ready for use.

Sitting there, I can hear the raucous voices of the men in friendly, but heated conversations. Everyone has gathered around our tack, anxious for the evening meal ahead. Mr. Frank and Uncle JT brought in some hamburgers, french fries and baked beans from a local diner, and it smells so good.

Turning the corner, Dad catches sight of me and says out, "Lee, come over here. You hungry?"

Boy am I. The monster that is hunger within my stomach is eating at my intestines and the salty smell of the hamburgers, fries and baked beans calls to me. The scent alone lays tale to its taste I can imagine so definitively and even before eating it, I know it will fill me up.

I walk up to Dad and he gives me a big hug, grasping his arms around my much smaller body. I can feel his own fatigue, but also a sense of calmness I have never before seen. I smile up at him and as he looks back at me he says, "I'm proud of you son. You done good today."

I shy away from the praise, but realize he is not saying it to placate me or to serve my character. Instead, I see the words give him a sense of pride. The opportunity to tell me... the reason for telling me perhaps means more to him than the words themselves.

I grab a large paper plate and Uncle Bill, who was in euphoric conversation with Dad before my arrival, picks up one of the burgers and a heaping hand full of french fries, along with a ladle filled with baked beans and places them onto my plate. He then says, "I don't think this will rival your Momma's cookin'… but it'll do."

After sitting back down on another cardboard beer box, I place the plate on my lap, reach for another pop from the cooler beside me and begin to dig into the feast. While doing so, my concentration holds firm to the horsemen, nearly the entire group of them now, all huddled around our tack.

A soft harmonica whistles in the background courtesy of Pigtail, one of the Stivers' brothers, as the conversation holds everyone's attention. These men are all like brothers, and for most of them, competition is the only time they can all get together.

With cars being the only means of reliable transportation, it is difficult for everyone to visit during the off-times between competitions. Most of these men are spread all over Ohio, Pennsylvania, Kentucky, Indiana, Virginia, Missouri and Tennessee, and traveling those distances on a consistent basis is just not feasible. The weekends of the competitions are the only time to meet and rekindle relationships, learn about the other camps and more importantly, about the lives of their 'brothers'.

What made this fraternity so extraordinary was the fact that there are so few black men in this profession nationwide, but here it is different. The Mighty Middletown Horsemen are all black men.

Their actions with working the horses were well known and later I found out, even legendary. These were exceptional men who trained exceptional horses but never received credit, or recognition for it. However, for most of them it did not matter at all. Instead, all that did matter were the horses being taken care of and performing at their best.

As I ate my burger, I sat quietly and listened to these men interact. In this time, I learned more about these horsemen than I ever had before.

Chapter 5

The evening colors of dusk start to fade away, closing the book on yet another day. However, this day has not been like any other for me. Here I am, surrounded by the since forgotten horsemen. Men who were so instrumental in their time, yet years later, have nary a sentence linked to their names in the history books.

Their legend rests not just in horses, but in American society itself. For their clique was formed of the best the 1950's had to offer. And there was no membership or initiation that held this elite group together, but instead, a solid love for the horses and an oblivious disregard for society's framework that at the time would have them otherwise work even more behind the scenes. And here I am, with the opportunity to watch them firsthand.

As I sit eating my dinner and admiring all the tack displayed around us, I listen intently, although not so obviously, to the conversations running through the circle.

"So Tom," Beauford Hall says out from the ring of men around the tack toward Dad, "You ever make it down to 'Nooga with Bachtel to see about that new stallion he was thinkin' 'bout?"

Upon hearing the words, Dad turns his head. The question catches me off guard. Dad never mentioned even considering going to Chattanooga, yet in this realm, it is small talk.

"Naw," Dad replies, "that stallion was from Runaway King's stock, so there ain't no way he is a bad horse. And I don't care how temperamental the horse is… it can be trained."

"Ain't that the truth," Bulgia chimes in, as the rest of the men nod in agreement.

"Yeah, no sense in making the trip, so I just told Doc if he looked good to him, he was good to me," Dad adds.

Collectively, the horsemen form their own society. In the real world, each black man would be forced to take a back seat to their white counterparts, but not here. Among them, all were equal… and all were proud. Their skill with American Saddlebreds literally would change the history of the breed. At the time, no one could see the impact they were having, but it was there nonetheless.

"Runaway King," Stanley Jackson then adds, "Ain't that the horse that won the *five* in like four shows in a row a few years ago?"

"I hear he comes from Sherman's horse Lexington," another voice says, too quickly for me to pick up the origin from.

"All good horses come from Lexington," Dad replies proudly, "And any horse that can carry a name like that has to have some of the finest blood in it."

" Did Bachtel ever pick up that stallion then? If not, I may have to tell Miller about him," Pretty Boy finally joins in. My eyes catch his, but he does not seem to notice.

"Charles Miller?" Bulgia retorts, "Shit, that white man wouldn't know a good horse if it bit him on the ass."

"That's why he needs me!"

All the men begin to break into a collective chuckle and I start to see a pattern arise. Although they have not seen each other for awhile, they are like family... brothers even. It is as if the time apart has only been a few days and their bond never skips a beat.

As the laughter calms down, Pretty Boy then adds, "Seriously though, did he?"

Looking over, Dad replies, "Naw Pete... I don't think so. Why, you all need a new horse?"

"We need something to bring some fresh blood into these competitions! I know what to expect from all of you, I've seen all ya 'alls horses so much."

"Hell," Dan Brown adds, "that's the truth. Seems at times we go round 'n round."

"Hah," Uncle JT then chimes in, "but you should know by now you don't stand a chance when Tom and me are around."

"That may be true if Tom would ever show a horse," Pretty Boy counters. "But we all know why he don't. Hell, we all know why none of you don't. That's your loss though."

To me, those sounded like fighting words, but they did not even seem to bother my dad. He let it roll off his back but Uncle Bill would have none of it. The crowd knows Pretty Boy stepped over a line, but from the stories Dad told me of him, that was common.

Nonetheless, Uncle Bill came to Dad's defense, "You know nothing about why he does or does not show horses. You have your head stuck so far up Miller's ass... that's the only reason you show. And if I recall, even doing so you ain't ever beat one of Tom's horses head to head."

The crowd laughs at Uncle Bill's comment, but for a moment I feel like the tension is still thick. Then diffusing the situation, Pete smiles and chucks a piece of bread at Dad and says, "Hah, ya know Tom... I think he's right goddammit! That's all gonna change this weekend though. We got us some fine horses competing this weekend. That's for sure."

As I eat and sip on the pop, I continue to listen to the conversations.

" Any of you seen the new Glory yet?" asks Eddie Stivers, who thus far has been the quietest of the bunch.

For the moment, I am lost by his question. But not wanting to seem as such, I just look down at my plate and continue eating.

"Yeah I have," his brother William answers, taking a moment to stop playing on his mouth harp.

"I still can't get over it," Stanley Jackson adds. "I mean... a new state. What the hell we gonna do with Alaska anyways?"

"Who knows, but looking to take a trip up there soon," Ted Morris says, taking a moment from his own dinner to get a word in.

"Why the hell you wanna go up there?" Pretty Boy chimes in, "Ain't nothin' but a damn iceberg."

"You think I like the Kentucky summers? They are hot as hell."

"Also," Tom Butler says, "I hear the fishin' is real good up there... real good."

"Exactly," Ted agrees, "See, Tom knows."

"Well," Dad then adds in himself as he looks up toward the grandstand of the fairgrounds, barely viewable now as the night's darkness has enveloped the area. "It don't look like Canfield has gotten in the new flags yet..."

"Has it even been finished?" Uncle Bill asks.

"It ain't official yet... naw, I don't think so," Uncle JT counters.

"The flag may not be official, but it sure as hell should be. How many ways can you add a new star to it?" Pretty Boy retorts.

"Yeah," Dad then adds, "I hear they may be waiting on releasing a new design because Hawaii is officially gonna be part of the U.S. too."

Listening to these men talk current events is a little odd for me. In my mind's eye, I always envisioned them living and breathing horses, forgetting that they each lived actual lives and had interests beyond their horses.

For Dad, Uncle JT and Uncle Bill, I have seen them relaxing, living life, but for the rest of these men the only stories I have heard were those that were horse related. This opportunity was rare and exciting, having the opportunity to see how they viewed the world. It was something that I could never have explained to me without actually viewing first hand.

"Now Hawaii," Uncle JT says, "That's a place I would love to go. Talk about fishin'... and the sun... and the beautiful women."

"Yeah Ted... do they even have women up in Alaska?" Pretty Boy teases with a chuckle.

Shooting a glare in Pete's direction, Ted responds, "You a funny man now Pretty Boy?"

"You know," Tom Butler then adds, "They say horses came here by way of Alaska originally, across the... Bearing Strait I think they call it."

"What the hell are you talking about?" Pretty Boy then goads on, always the talkative one. "What the hell is the Bearing Strait?"

"Didn't you go to school Boy?" Uncle Bill replies. "The Strait connects Alaska to Russia, or somewhere over there. They say it used to be a land bridge or something."

"I tell you what. Ain't a Kentucky mare that ever came from any Russian iceland. I can promise you that!" blurts out Pretty Boy.

Pretty Boy shakes his head in disbelief and for the rest of the group there is a moment of silence. Dad walks over to the record player and as he begins to fiddle with it, Eddie Stivers breaks the quiet, "Forget about Alaska. I wanna hear more about Hawaii."

"They say if it becomes a state anytime soon, the 49 star flag will be short lived, so a lot of factories are waiting to see what happens,"Beauford Hall replies.

"I don't wanna hear 'bout no flag," laughs out Eddie, "I wanna hear about the women."

Ain't that the truth, the rest of the men mumble together, grins encompassing their faces. "So tell us JT... tell us about the women over there on those islands."

"Me?" Uncle JT answers with a surprise. "What the hell do I know about Hawaiian women?"

"What the hell does he know about any woman?" Pretty Boy laughs out, interrupting with a shout.

Eddie lets out a slight snicker before continuing on, "Well. Ain't you from an island or something?"

"Man... I'm Jamaican, not Hawaiian. Shit..."

Instantly we all erupt into a hardy laughter after Uncle JT's proclamation. Having been around these men for awhile, I now understand that for all the ribbing, the tone is very friendly. For all their differences and the pressure of competition, underneath they truly all enjoy each other's company.

Just then, Will Stivers once again lays off his harmonica to speak, "Man, from what I hear, their bodies are tanned dark and their asses are firm and tight from all that dancing."

The men all nod in approval as Bulgia then adds in, "And all they do all day is lay around in their bikinis and hulas. And there must be five women to every one man!"

Laughing in disbelief, Uncle Bill then asks, "Where the hell you hear that Bulgia?"

"I saw it in that Elvis movie, *King Creole.*"

"Man, that shit ain't real!" Pretty Boy laughs out. "What are you doing watching an Elvis movie?"

"I like that white boy," Bulgia replies, "He has himself some real down south soul."

At that moment, Dad puts down the needle of the player onto a spinning record. After a moment of scratching, the needle flattens out and begins to transmit the sound. Dad lifts his arms to his waist and begins snapping his fingers as the music starts playing.

"Darling you send me, I know you send me, Darling you send me, honest you do, honest you do, Honest you do, whoa-oh-oh-oh-oh-oh," Dad sings out in conjunction with the song.

On that note, a few of the men stand up and all together they begin to sing along, "You thrill me, I know you, you, you thrill me. Darling you, you, you, you thrill me, honest you do."

By this time, William Stivers is in full accompaniment on his Horner as the men all continue on together in step with the rhythmic gospel and blues echoing from the player. "At first I thought it was infatuation, but woo, it's lasted so long. Now I find myself wanting to marry you and take you home, whoa –oh-oh- oh-oh-oh. You, you, you, you send me, I know you send me, I know you send me, Honest you do."

As the men all surround each other, they are now standing in a full circle. Then, in the loudest voices possible, the men sing in harmony the ending of the song, "I know, I know, I know, you send me, I know you send me, Whoa-oh-oh-oh, you, you, you, you send me, honest you do…"

Upon its completion, the men burst out into a common laughter and their bond is obvious.

"Now that Sam Cooke," Uncle Bill yells out, "Now that man has himself some soul!"

"Ain't that the truth," Pretty Boy agrees with a finger snap. "What do you think Bulgia?"

"Man no one sings soul like ole Sam," Bulgia replies aloud before toning himself down to add, "But I still like that white boy too."

Pretty Boy laughs out as he gives Bulgia a hug and the men all sit back down. Our meals have long been finished and time has passed by in the hours, although it feels like it has only been a few minutes.

I find myself lost in the fun and unknowingly, I begin to

rekindle an old habit I try my best to repress, especially around these men. During the reunion together, Uncle Bill sees me sucking my thumb, a habit I picked up in my younger years and seemed to resurface whenever not actively engaged in something.

Seeing this and not wanting me to embarrass myself, he comes over and says, "How would you like a dollar boy?"

Looking up and not even noticing what I am doing, I reply with wide eyes, "Yes sir!" I enjoyed having money given to me, so without hesitation, I took my thumb out of my mouth and outstretched my hands to receive my bounty. I quickly learned though that there was a catch.

Uncle Bill takes a dollar and wraps it around my left thumb and secures it with a rubber band and tells me, "Now boy, if ya don't remove the dollar for the rest of the evening, it's yours to keep."

Seeing this, Dad nods in approval. Never one to miss an opportunity, Pretty Boy says, "I got a dollar that says he don't make it."

The rest of the men all begin chattering away, placing their money on both sides of the possible outcome. On my side though, I see Dad placing a bet in my favor, knowing I would make it through the evening.

"Easy money for both of us," he whispers in my ear as he gives me a strong hug.

For the next few minutes, the chattering slows down and the

men seem to be lost in Sam Cooke's voice, which is still echoing through the speaker, but now is a song I am unfamiliar with.

"Ya know what," Bulgia says to the group.

"What's that?" Stanley Jackson asks.

"The soul in Sam's voice. Reminds me of the Big Bopper."

"Now what the hell are you talking about," Pretty Boy says with his eyebrow raised, "What is it with you and these white boys? He don't sound nothin' like Sam Cooke."

"I'm not saying they sound alike. I'm saying the soul in them reminds me of him."

"Shit..." Pretty Boy says with a shake of his head, as he brings the cup of Kentucky Bourbon he had been cradling up to his lips.

"It's a damn shame he had to die like he did," Bulgia adds.

"Mr. Jones' daughter," Ted Morris says, "was a big Richie Valens fan. I think she cried for a week over that. Some sad stuff."

In agreement, the tone of the conversation quiets as all the men recall the events in their head. Even I knew of that night, 'The Day the Music Died'. I know for a fact Mr. Jones' daughter wasn't the only one who cried.

Wanting to lighten the conversation, something which he seemed to be good at, Pretty Boy speaks up, "So you all ready for this weekend? Should be a tough competition with all you here."

"Yeah, we are definitely ready," Uncle JT replies. "But it

won't be in our hands. We can only take the horses so far. The owners show the horses, that's just the way it is. Except of course where you're concerned. I gotta ask ya' Pete, why do you show the horses?"

"You'd think all the shit I take from you all would shy me away from it, but I like the excitement," Pretty Boy responds. "On top of that, I get an extra bill every horse I ride. Hell, for that kinda green who wouldn't do it? I look at it like this. I get paid to do a job, and that job is winning. That's all the owners care about, so it's all I can care about. If I don't win, they'll get a trainer that can. And I sure as hell don't want my livelihood resting on the skill of these white folk. Not a damn one of these owners can hold a candle to our riding. Nope... no sir. Not a damn one of 'em. That's my opinion at least."

Bulgia, after having a few sips of bourbon from his flask, then speaks up about the differences between them and the horse owners, "Hell, the owners would be nothing without us. They wouldn't even be able to sit on the horses if not for our training. Sometimes it makes me sick. We get no recognition for the work we do. None at all."

"Its not about recognition," Dad interjects, "We do it for the love of the horses and to feed our families."

"Look," Bulgia then replies, "I love the horses too and all. But the bottom line is the owners are rich and we're not. They're white like buttermilk, and we're brown like chocolate and in the end, we're nothin' but a few pieces of chocolate chips in a bucket of buttermilk."

Just as Bulgia begins to repeat slowly and emphatically his words as he shakes his head, "We're nothin' but," all the men join in concluding the phrase, "a few pieces of chocolate chips in a bucket of buttermilk," practically preaching the gospel of the phrase.

It was a statement they had shared amongst themselves often and although they would laugh with pride while saying the words, underneath the laughter there is some concern about the reality of their life. The truth is something they are all aware of, but on the surface they find a way to let it go.

By nine o'clock it is time for bed. Each of the horsemen go their separate way, ready to sleep in preparation of an early and eventful morning. Grabbing me by the arm, Dad helps me up and pulls back the tack drape to our sleeping stall. Inside, there are three small single cots for Dad, Uncle JT and me, right next to the horses. It isn't much, but because of my exhaustion I welcome its limited comfort.

My first day was a success. It started in the early morning and as I drift off to sleep now, I recount what I learned. My day was not so much about the horses, although they have been around me the entire time, but instead, it has been an education on existence.

I learned more about life, the horsemen and the camaraderie of their own private society than I ever thought possible. I caught a glimpse into a world I so admired. And as I drifted off to sleep, my thoughts rested on the great evening, my soul hummed to the smooth voice of Sam Cooke and my inner man imagined myself fishing in Alaska with a beautiful island girl dancing beside me. I am happy.

And for the record, I made it through the evening a dollar richer.

Chapter 6

Friday

Early the next morning, my night's dreams are interrupted by Dad's voice. Resting happily underneath my dark blue wool blanket, I long for the comfort to remain. However, in the back of my mind, I know it won't.

Turning over, I position myself onto my back and stretch out my legs. The thick cover is pulled up to just under my nose and in a haze I slowly open my eyes, trying to make sense of my unfamiliar surroundings.

As my vision starts to come into focus, I see Dad before me and I begin to regain my bearings.

"C'mon Lee. Time to get up. We got a big day ahead of us."

For a ten year old, the very idea of waking up at 4:30 in the morning, when the air is still cold as winter solstice and the sky is still as black as coal is incomprehensible. But this is not about me and my fatigue and with that thought in my mind, I exhale a deep breath and swing my legs around off the edge of the cot.

With the blanket still covering my lap, I rub my eyes as the sleep trails away from my clouded head. Involuntarily, my mouth opens wide with a yawn and the sound accompanying it sounds like a foghorn.

Off to the side, I hear Uncle JT laughing up a storm, but trying to keep it under wraps. However, I know his humor is directed at me and to be honest, I feel the same way inside. For all my talk, the early morning is a lot tougher than I imagined it to be.

"Need any more sleep? Or you gonna be ok?" Dad asks me with a smile of his own.

"Naw," I reply as I stand up and stretch my arms back, arching my back to awaken my spine, "I'll be fine."

"Good, good. We'll be busy today."

I know Dad's words are true. Before the sun even fully rises, the horses need to be fed and watered. Beyond that, I have no idea what chores I will have, but I can only imagine they will seem never-ending. The preparation required to place well in these competitions is immense.

"Just get the boy a cup a jo'… and he'll be good to go!" Uncle JT exclaims.

I look up toward Dad thinking Uncle JT may be right. I can't recall ever having coffee before, but it just *sounds* like it'll hit the spot. Moreover, as much as I hated leaving the warm blanket, I hated even more the thought of disappointing my dad. And if the java will help remove the morning grogginess, I am all for it.

As that thought fades from my mind, Dad hands me a warm washcloth. The wet cotton is quickly losing its steam in the frigid morning air and not wasting any time, I place it upon my face.

The semi-warm wetness of the cloth awakens my senses and I find relief in it. It helps rejuvenate my soul and almost instantly, I become more prepared to handle the early hours.

Standing, I fold up the blanket on my bed. In a few short minutes, I change my clothes to match the new day and clean myself up a bit.

After getting ready, I pull back the cloth to our stable 'room' and head outside to the fire-pit beside the southern barn's concession stand. My senses catch the fine smell of flapjacks on the griddle and beside that I notice a cauldron of oatmeal. My stomach yearns for the food and eagerly, I grab myself a plate.

" How did you sleep son?" Uncle Bill asks me, as I find him standing in line next to me.

"It was good. Still a little tired though," I reply as I fill my plate.

"These early mornings will do that to ya. Why don't you get yourself a cup of coffee? It'll wake you right up."

"Yeah, that's what Uncle JT was saying. I think I might." With that, I give a nod goodbye and head over to the coffee. I look around, but no one seems inclined to stop me. So with a shrug, I fill up a mug and then move over to the edge of the barn and find a seat among the rest of the men. Unlike last night, the crowd is made up of only the men whose stables share our barn.

As such, the talk filling the morning air is more geared to the business at hand, the competitions of the weekend.

"How many horses you bring this time Tom?" Uncle Bill asks.

"Six. We are running two horses each in the three, five, and fine harness. I like our chances."

"What is it with you and the Dells Farm and the gaits anyway?" Pretty Boy chimes in from off near the griddle.

"Don't you know," Uncle JT says out jubilantly. "That's where all the prestige is."

"It won't matter anyways. Mark my words. I gaur-un-tee a victory in the gait. I sure do," Pretty Boy replies with a strong affirmation.

"I wouldn't doubt you," Dad interjects. "You have yourself some damn good horses."

"Thank you Tom," Pretty Boy says with a smile. "I'll remember your kindness in the winner's circle."

"I know you will Boy... I know you will," Dad replies with a smile, tongue in cheek.

After a bit more conversation, all the men finish their meals and clean up. Dawn is within the hour and now that we have been fed, it is time to do the same for the horses. Even though it is still dark out, the fairgrounds are bustling. The sleep within me has completely faded and now I find myself eager to get my chores started.

Following my meal and taking my plate to the cleaning cart, I decide to take a swallow of the hot, thick coffee of which I have been slow to try. With my mouth dry and in need of some liquid 'life', I hold the ceramic mug in both hands and feel its warmth against my skin. Then, throwing trepidation to the wind, I bring the cup to my mouth, tip it back and let the java flow into my throat.

The foul taste experience was not as expected. I was imagining it to taste like chocolate, with perhaps a nutty undertone. Instead, I likened it to black tar. Now, I've never tasted tar before, but I have smelt hot asphalt and the smell that comes with it is repulsive. This is similar. Thicker than I expected and wrapped in a burnt undercurrent, the coffee goes down like a load of bricks and about knocks me to the ground. My nose cringes as I put the cup down and turn my head in disgust.

Off behind me, I can hear the group chuckling at my reaction. I am a bit embarrassed, but boy, does it taste rough. Just then, Dad comes over and says, "Son, black is fine for many things, but not for your first cup of coffee. You need some suggah and milk in that."

He then brings my cup over to the serving cart, and throws in two large spoonfuls of sugar and pours in a stream of milk. Then, using the same spoon he served the sugar with, he mixes it up.

The black coffee turns a light brown and almost instantly, seems more delectable. With a smile he hands it to me while saying, "There ya go. Why don't you give this a try?"

I take the cup from him and with a bit more apprehension than the last time, I bring it once more to my lips and kick it back. This time, the liquid goes down smooth. My taste buds, though not embracing the coffee, no longer reject it and I fill my body with the remainder of the cup.

"Better?" Dad asks with a wink.

"Much!"

"Good, now let's get to work. Those horses have got to be getting real hungry."

On that statement, we go back to the stable. Dad walks over to the same hi-fi player nestled just inside the front entrance to the barn and puts on the 45 single of Jerry Butler and the Impressions song, *For Your Precious Love*. After the familiar scratching of the needle on vinyl, Jerry Butler's smooth silky voice comes through the large audio speaker.

Music always played a big part in the world of these horsemen. Dad often talked about how the horses were very much like men, loving the sounds of music and recognizing the beauty and calmness of certain songs. He added that horses could think and feel similarly to people, and music simply made them feel better. He would say that the horses loved our music and "who in the world, be it man, woman or horse doesn't like the fine voice of Sam Cooke, Johnny Mathis, Fats Domino and that young boy Ray Charles." He referred to music as having the greatest calming effect on the horses and trainers as well. As a result, if you would walk into any stable of the Mighty Middletown Horsemen, you would be treated to some smooth sounds on the hi-fi. It's just the way it was.

Soon Dad, Uncle JT and this time myself included are singing along with the popular hit. At the chorus, Uncle JT picks up a pitchfork and begins to move around with it, mimicking dancing with a woman. The entire time he is serenading to the barn tool, telling it all his love is for her, and that's what love will do, all for her precious love.

Seeing this, Dad begins to laugh heartily. Then, in between the chuckles he says out, "No wonder you're having troubles courtin' Kat. Look how you hold that pitchfork! Let me show you how a woman is supposed to be held Country Boy!"

As he takes the pitchfork from Uncle JT and begins to move around with the farm tool he says, "A woman is like that horse," pointing to Painted Doll who is watching as intensely as we are. "Why do you think we call 'em both fine fillies? As Dad dances in a circle with both his arms wrapped around and embracing the pitchfork, and still singing *For Your Precious Love* he says, "You have to treat her gently, but firmly. Let her know you care. Listen to her breath and feel the music as you feel her... close to your heart. It's about the feeling man... it's all about feeling!"

At the end of the song, Dad hands the pitchfork back to Uncle JT and finishes off, "Now that's how it's done."

"Thanks Mojo," he laughs out in response. "I'll remember that and so will Painted Doll."

"Serve you well too," Dad replies as he nudges Uncle JT. Then in a loud voice he says, "Alright, we got a lot to do. Let's get to it."

Unsure exactly what to do myself, I move over toward my dad.

"O.k. Lee," he says to me. "Lets finally get these horses fed, watered and give them their morning workout. After that, we will give them a good brush down. Can you handle all that?"

"Yes sir," I reply energetically.

"Good, let's get to it. I'll start down on this end with Ambassador, you and JT start on that end with Painted Doll. If we each do three horses, it'll only take half the time."

After quickly moving toward the bundled hay, Uncle JT and I grab a large sack and carry it over to the horses. As we place the bundle on the ground, Uncle JT whips out his 440 American Eagle buck knife and with a flip of the wrist, releases the blade.

In a single motion, Uncle JT slices apart the cord holding the bundle together. Then carefully, we begin to place the hay in each stable. Afterwards, we check to make sure each horse has enough water to last until midday. Looking over, I see we have been keeping pace with Dad. I follow Uncle JT over to Hot Toddy and motion him out of his stable by pulling on his halter. Gently he follows me out and as he does, I clip on the reins. Uncle JT then mounts his bridle and together we exit for the large practice ring. Besides us and Dad with King Cloud, there are a few other horsemen who look like they are just finishing up. As we wait for our opening on the field, I admire the strength and majesty of our horses. With the tone accented by their dark pigment they look muscular and powerful, yet very graceful in motion in a poetic sort of way.

" How long do we exercise them for?" I ask as I pat Hot Toddy on his side.

"That's a damn good question," Uncle JT responds. "Surprisingly, most horses don't get enough exercise and when they finally do get exercise, they usually get too much. A good trainer will learn to find that balance. Add in the fact that we need them at their best for the competitions and there is a whole mess of things a trainer needs to think about."

"That's right," Dad adds. "These horses depend on us. They can't make their own decisions. We have to make sure they get what they need without overdoing it. Out in the wild a horse will walk, jog and lope as the mood strikes him. He'll travel about thirty miles in 24 hours. Of course, there are plenty of stops along the way for drinking, grazing and snoozing. In doing so, a horse will get himself fit for the job he is doing, which is surviving. And that will be that."

"But," Uncle JT says, adding to Dad's response, "In a cramped place like this, horses stand, walk in tiny circles, snooze, eat, drink and travel only a few miles in a day. After spending the bulk of their life in a twelve by twelve stall, we then ask these horses to show or just to zip around an arena for an hour. That's just abuse. So, exercising these guys right is real damn important."

Dad then continues on, "the trick is to not only race their heart, but let them know it is almost competition time. You see, what we are doing here is not just exercising the horses, but also practicing with them the events they are competing in. Luckily, all the horses we got with us here today have been in this atmosphere before. If they hadn't, we may end up doing this a bit different. King Cloud and Hot Toddy have been doing the five gait for a long while, so this is second nature to them. We'll just go ahead and work them through the five to give them a feel for it, preparing them for Doc."

As he finishes, he catches sight of the training ring, now vacant, and we move the two horses in. As Uncle JT and I stand off to the side with Hot Toddy in tow, Dad slowly climbs upon King Cloud. The horse nickers with a soft 'rat-ta-tat-tat' sound as if saying, "Hi, I'm glad you're here," while Dad settles into the saddle.

The five gait, which Dad starts to ride King Cloud through, is considered by many as the most spectacular and exciting of all the events in the show because of the speed and strength exhibited by these well-trained athletes. Five-Gaited horses such as King Cloud and Hot Toddy have long, flowing manes and tails and perform with an unparallel strength and grace. The five gait is broken up into five sections; the walk, trot, canter, slow gait and rack.

The slow gait, also sometimes called a 'stepping pace' which means that two legs on the same side of the animal move simultaneously, but the hind foot contacts the ground slightly before the front foot, and the rack, the most exciting gait of the five gaited horse, were inherited by the American Saddlebred from its ancestor, the Naragansett Pacer. Each foot hits the ground separately in a four-beat cadence. The rack should be performed at a speed that is comfortable for the rider.

In this competition, the trot used is a square, bold, two-beat gait performed with speed, form and natural, high action. The canter is slow, rhythmic and must be executed on the correct lead. The slow gait is a high action gait, performed slowly, while the rack is fast, showing action, energy and power. The walk is springy and athletic. The best performer maintains good form and balance, even at speed.

Over the next twenty minutes or so, I watch as Dad and King Cloud practice the nuances of the five gait. I become lost in the sight of Dad on the horses. I did not realize it at the time, but that memory became forever entrenched in my mind's eye. His poise and strength became even more apparent when atop a horse and one could sense the inner joy and peace it brought him.

After finishing riding King Cloud, Dad hops off the horse and then walks over to Hot Toddy to the kind words of praise from a few men.

"Nice ride, Mojo," Uncle JT shouts out.

Never one for wanting attention, he blushes coyly even if appreciative of their adulation. Then, in a fluid motion he rises on to the saddle of the second horse.

As Dad sets aboard Hot Toddy, he pulls me up on the saddle in front of him and demonstrates to me how to hold the reins. He places his titanium, iron-like hands with their intense veins protruding from all the years of firmly gripping tethered reins and farm work, and wraps them over mine and maneuvers my fingers to interweave with the leather. His hands are calloused from never wearing gloves while working and his skin is rough and coarse.

He then speaks to me about how each movement of the reins helps 'shake the bit' resulting in the different commands used to control the horse. Years later, this technique was further explained to me by an old-time horseman who told me that because American Saddlebreds are versatile and easy to train, a great trainer can also get a 'man-made' or well-trained horse to change movements of the gait by the simple 'shaking the bit' technique Dad showed me. As Dad would say, a horse can feel and think as good as any human and this technique was a testament to that.

After showing me, he helps me off Hot Toddy and then proceeds to post him through his techniques, and speaks to the horse in a calming way, reminding himself that horses must be treated like children with a lot of tender love and care. I can not help but wonder how Dad can read horses so magically. When I watch him ride Hot Toddy, I can see he is content; lost within a world only he and the other horsemen could understand. It seems as if he goes to a place that most people can only dream of. With that comes a peace of mind that transcends the boundaries of an inequitable life he and his fellow black horsemen had to overcome.

After finishing, Dad lowers his head and places his ear next to Hot Toddy's and whispers inaudibly. His words obviously have an effect on him as he snorts delicately in approval. Dad then jumps down off Hot Toddy and hands me the reins. Uncle JT and I follow Dad and King Cloud back to the barn and leash the two horses outside their stalls. Thirsty, I get myself some water and ask, "What's next?"

" You tired yet or you ready for some more?" Dad responds.

"I'm good."

"Alright then, because we still have a lot of work ahead of us, right JT?"

"Sure is the truth there. We need to bathe and towel dry the horses, and then give them a good brushing after that," Uncle JT responds.

"Think you can handle all that?" Dad asks me.

"Yeah, just show me what to do," I reply, excited to get started on the next task.

To bathe the horses, we first move them one at a time off to a large, grassy section of the fairgrounds close to our barn. By bathing the horses on a grassy pasture, we minimize any chance of mud forming on the ground while we wash them. Washing down a horse can be a messy task, but given the midday heat which is intensifying, getting wet while bathing the horses will be refreshing.

As I hold the reins of King Cloud, Uncle JT starts the bathing process. He begins by wetting the entire body, down to the skin. Given the hot, humid weather, it is easy to tell King Cloud is enjoying the cool attention. He spreads the water upon him, starting at the feet and working his way up his body.

"You know why I start here," Uncle JT asks me as he pours the water upon King Cloud.

"No sir. Not exactly," I respond, but honestly wanting to know.

"Well, it eases him into the bath. The feel and sound of the water… it's a lot like easing your way into a lake."

"Don't you just jump right in?" I ask back with a smile.

"Well boy, I suppose most people do. But we don't want King Cloud jumping no where."

After he is all watered down, Uncle JT starts to sponge on some soapy water, rubbing it in deep into King Cloud's coat. He seems to really enjoy it, because for a moment I can see a smile on his elongated face. The calmness in his eyes is soothing and I must admit, I find the entire process a bit relaxing.

Once he is done rubbing him down, Uncle JT rinses King Cloud off, massaging him as the soapy water melds into the ground below.

"Why don't you go fetch us a couple towels? You can help me dry him down," Uncle JT says to me as he grabs the reins.

Eager to be involved, I turn back into the barn and grab a few towels from our tack. Within fifteen minutes, King Cloud is all clean and dry from our efforts and careful to keep him as such, we move him back to his stable. We then repeat the entire process with Hot Toddy.

"Are we gonna do this to all the horses?" I ask.

"Yeah, but not until after we work out each one. We need the horses looking their best you know," Uncle JT responds.

"That's right," Dad says, having just returned back from grabbing us all a quick lunch from the concession stand. "You two hungry?" he then asks with a grin.

As Uncle JT and I dig in to the hot dogs, chips and pop, Dad examines our handiwork. "Good job there son," he says to me while shooting a wink at Uncle JT. "You ready for some more? We still gotta brush them."

"Yes Dad," I respond as I scarf down the second half of my hot dog and wash it down with a swig of the cold pop.

"Alright then. Now we give the horses a brush down. But," Dad says to me, "There is more to brushing a horse than just brushing you know…"

For a moment, I am confused. Back home when told to brush the horse, that's all I ever did. "Umm… what do you mean?"

" This is competition time. We need to take extra care of the horses. Let's review some things I've told you before. First off, do you remember what side to approach from?"

Laughing slightly at the ease of the question I respond, "Of course. The left side, right?"

"Right," he says to me. "Now, you'll want to next move your hand down the horse's left front leg like this and gently squeeze the back of the fetlock."

"Fetlock?" I ask, forgetting the terminology.

"It's kind of like the horse's ankle. Right here," he answers me, pointing to the joint on the horse just above the hoof."

"Ahhh… I remember now."

"Then, pick up the horse's hoof so that you're looking at the bottom of it." After doing just that, he pulls out a long, silver pick from his back pocket. Looking at me he then adds, "Most of us horsemen carry one of these around with us. It makes your life a bit easier. Now, using the hoof pick, clean out the dirt in the hoof with a downward motion from the heel to the toe. It is important you do all four hooves."

He shows me the motion and after completing the first hoof, lets me work on the back one on the same side.

"Good," he says to me as I finish up. "You have a nice stroke. Hot Toddy likes you a lot."

The compliment makes me proud and it seems to focus my attention even more.

As Uncle JT finishes up the other two hooves, Dad says next, "Now go grab us a couple of those dandy brushes from the table."

While I return with the brushes Dad continues without missing a beat, "I want you to brush the horse's body with this brush to remove sweat and any dirt marks. Remember to use short strokes in the direction of the lie of the coat."

In demonstration, Dad presses the brush against the horse's coat and pulls it back toward him in a slow and short motion. He repeats the process a few times before continuing on, "When you're done, brush the legs, head, neck, mane and tail with the softer body brush. You can also use the body brush on the rest of the horse's body for a finished look. They really enjoy the feel of it."

"Got it," I say as I wait to get started.

"Good. Now, after all that, you'll have to go get a damp sponge to clean what?"

"The horse's eyes, nostrils and lips," I proudly reply.

"Good!" Dad exclaims. "But also, make sure you use a different sponge to clean under his dock."

"Dock?" I ask, again unsure of where that is on the horse.

Smiling, Dad replies, "The tail…"

"Gotchya," I say. "Is that it?"

"Yes, but the key points to remember and I trust you have, are these." Dad then squats down to look me directly in the eye and says, "One, talk softly to the horse as you work. Two, when touching a horse's rear, talk to the horse first and run your hand along his body from front to back to avoid startling him. Three, hold the tail when you brush the rear to keep the horse from kicking. Four, when brushing the tail, stand to the horse's side, not directly in back of him. Five, never sit or kneel on the floor to reach the lower parts. Instead, just squat or bend. Six, don't brush too hard, especially on the delicate legs and face. And seven... never, ever stand directly behind a horse. Do you remember that... you got all that?"

"Yup, I sure do. I think I do at least."

"You'll be fine. Remember, *just feel the horse* and you'll take good care of him. No doubt in my mind. Just listen to him and he'll let you know when you are doing something wrong."

With that, he pats me on the shoulder and begins walking down to the other end of the stable line. Then looking back he says, "You work with JT and start with Hot Toddy there, and I'll start work on King Cloud."

"Sounds good to me," I reply as I look Hot Toddy in his eyes. They are large and dark, and so full of gentle emotion. I find myself lost within his majesty and calmness. Leaning in, I whisper softly to him, "O.k. boy. Don't hate me if I get this wrong. I'll do my best."

As if understanding me completely, Hot Toddy turns his long neck and rubs the side of his face against mine. The nuzzle makes me giggle, showing my age, but I don't care. I find myself in a link with the horse and just as Dad said, *feel* him as I begin working on him.

Chapter 7

It takes us over twenty minutes to properly 'brush' the two horses, but the time passes as if only a few minutes go by. I find myself lost in a mutual relationship with them, one of trust and understanding.

As I am finishing up, I see a tall white man enter through the front of the barn doors. He looks familiar and quickly I recognize him as Dr. Bachtel. I watch him intently, half hiding behind the horse I am brushing. Upon entering, he catches sight of me and approaches.

In his mid-fifties, he walks with a subtle arrogance familiar in people with wealth and fame. His pale and pasty white skin is accented by his graying brown hair and thick eyebrows.

While oncoming from the right side, he pats Hot Toddy and in a high-pitched voice unbecoming of his height says to me, "Hello Lee. Good to see you here boy. How are you doing?"

"Good sir," I reply.

"Excited for the weekend? Should be a good competition don't you think? Speaking of which, is your daddy around?"

Dr. Bachtel gained his wealth as a veterinarian and owned the farm that Dad worked on. His love of horses though was not nearly at the same level as Dad's. Instead, Dr. Bachtel was involved in competitions such as these for bragging rights, a common trait I was told among the wealthy owners. However, I never heard Dad say anything negative or bad about his boss, but in all honesty, he rarely had anything good to say either.

As Dr. Bachtel looks at me, smiling with a cigarette burning slow in hand, I give him the answer he is waiting for, "He'll be right back sir. He just went to use the john."

The smoke from the lit tobacco trails methodically into my nostrils and that of the horses. In annoyance, we both let out restrained snorts. My eyes stay firm on the man the entire time as he pats the horse half-heartedly and I silently pray for Dad to hurry up. My prayers are answered almost immediately as Dad comes into the stable.

"Hello Tom," Dr. Bachtel says.

The voice catches Dad off guard and looking up, his demeanor instantly changes from loose and relaxed to more business oriented, serious and professional.

"Hello Doc," Dad replies with a layer of true respect. "I wasn't expecting you so early."

"I hope I'm not bothering you."

"No sir. Not at all. Just getting ready for the competitions. Lot of tough horses out there this weekend."

"Yes, I was noticing just that on my way in. How do you think we will do?"

"I think we have a good shot. You got yourself here some damn good horses. You should be proud."

"I am Tom. I am. But a horse is only as good as its trainer. You do good work."

After shying away from the compliment, Dad finally replies courteously, "Thank you Doc."

Dad has always said Dr Bachtel is a good man who is polite to everyone, regardless of creed or color. In comparison to the rest of the real world, even in my youth I knew such a relationship was rare. Given the current events, perhaps Dr. Bachtel is ahead of his contemporaries in regards to race relations. Sure he needed my dad, but unlike some of the other owners, he showed his appreciation for the work of the often forgotten horsemen such as my dad and his colleagues. Granted, he never perceived Dad as an equal, but he did reciprocate the respect my dad showed him. Maybe it is because of his work in medicine as a veterinarian. It takes a gentle nature to work with animals and that nature surely transcends to other forms of life. I am unsure if Dr. Bachtel is a pro-civil rights believer and I doubt he is any type of activist, but he does lead by example. He seems to not only comprehend, but appreciate Dad's life as a fellow man and his trade and skill with the horses. Their love for the horses, even if born of different origins, was definitely the foundation of a bond between the two, enabling them to work together as successfully as they do.

In all, from the talks I've had with Dad, his feelings toward Dr. Bachtel are generally ambivalent. On one hand, he is very appreciative of the opportunity to ride and train the horses, especially since it enables him to use his love and skill to provide for his family. This in turn led to a mutual respect each man had for another, yet Dad quietly questioned Dr. Bachtel's commitment to his horses. This lack of dedication was accented by his average riding ability and often held the Dells from more victories than it should have received. Now, Dad would never say such a thing aloud, but he did not have to. The other horsemen, those of different camps and therefore with no ties to Dr. Bachtel often reminded him of that very fact. However, Dad always refrained from riding the horses in competition. He left that to Dr. Bachtel and accepted loss or victory as it came.

"Really Tom, how do you think we'll do this time around?"

"That's tough to say Doc. For all his talk, Pretty Boy is doing a hell'a…"

"Pretty Boy?" Dr. Bachtel interrupts.

"Sorry. Pete Jones is his name, out of Miller Farm."

"Right… Pete Jones, with Charles Miller. Charlie puts a lot of money into his horses."

"And it shows," Dad replies. "Pretty Bo… um, I mean Pete Jones, has been working real hard. He'll be hard to beat. Other than that, as you know, we have the Cambridge horses, the Founders horses, Pleasant Meadow, and Rogers Farms. All will be pretty tough."

"Wow, that sure sounds right. Those are all some pretty big farms we will be competing against."

" If I can say so myself Doc, we do a pretty good job here. If we make it to the money round in even one of the two gaits I think we can consider it a big victory considering the talent out here."

"I think you're right Tom. I really do. I'm really looking forward to riding these pretty horses."

"Well Doc, you're a good rider. Just remember to stay relaxed. These horses can sense your nervousness and respond in kind. But, if you are calm and in control, they respond to that too."

"You've always known a lot about horses. You ever think about saving up and showing your own horses?"

"No Doc, I'll leave the owning of the horses to people like you. Besides, it's a little too expensive for me."

"I hear you there. It does take some deep pockets. Well, you just make sure the horses are ready for me and Mrs. Bachtel."

"Don't I always," Dad says back with a smile of his own.

"Alright. Sounds good. I'll see you later Tom. The owners all have a little get together at the clubhouse. A little pre-competition jockeying if you know what I'm saying," he says with a friendly nudge.

"I understand. Us trainers do about the same thing. I'll make sure these horses are ready to do their best for ya."

"I know you will. Thanks."

As Dr. Bachtel begins to leave the stable, he reaches out and shakes my dad's hand. Then, turning around he makes his way over to me. This entire time I was trying to look busy, but I was still brushing the same spot on the same horse that I was when Dr. Bachtel came into the barn in the first place.

"Well Lee, Have you been working hard? Taking good care of my horses?"

"Yes sir I have been. Making sure they are fed and watered, exercised all right and polishing the tack."

"That is an important job. Remember, we have to look our best out there. The competition is stiff."

"You will have the cleanest horse out there." I reply, now pretty sure of myself.

"I'm gonna hold you to that," he says with a smile back at me. Then, reaching into his pocket, the doctor pulls out a one dollar bill. "Here you go," he says as he hands it to me. "This is your pay for the week. Don't let me down ok.?"

Upon seeing the money, a smile grows on my face spanning from ear to ear. "I will sir... I mean I won't sir... I mean I'll do you proud sir," I reply nervously.

"Very good. Keep up the work."

"I will sir. Thank you."

The excitement was not as much in the value of the money, but in what it represented. I had never before experienced the feeling of being hired and earning a salary. Sure, I had worked around the house, did my chores and received a Christmas allowance. But this is different. The same man who has hired and paid my dad was doing the same for me. I felt an immeasurable pride, and it was beaming from me like a lighthouse in a storm.

Some may think someone my age working and learning a work ethic so young to be rare, but for my brothers and me as well as other farm kids, it is just second nature. Dad instilled a work ethic in us at a young age. For instance, in the summers we would bail the hay from the acres of fields surrounding our house. I would sometimes drive the tractor with the bed truck attached and other times, Dad would drive while my brother, Harry, and I would lift the bails of hay from behind and load them onto the flat-bed carrier. When the flat-bed was full, we would return to the barn, unload and stack the bails in the hay loft and return to load more bails. We would do this all day long in the heat of summer. That was where my brother and I as kids learned our work ethic and this experience, getting paid first hand by Dr. Bachtel, just cemented it.

Seeing the joy on my face resulting from being paid by Dr. Bachtel brought with it a mixture of happiness and sadness for my dad. He later told me he was proud of the money I had earned, but he did not want it to alter my opinion of Dr. Bachtel or of the work involved in training horses. Dad never wanted me in the horse training business, but I was the only child of his six kids who took such an interest in the horses. However, as with every parent, he wanted more for me than training horses could offer and although right for him, it was not the fate he wanted for me.

As my euphoria is wearing down, Dad calls out to me, "Lee, grab Ambassador. JT is getting Next To My Heart... we gotta give them their work for the day."

Stuffing the dollar into my pocket, I respond with a grin and run over to the horse. Then, pulling him by his halter, I follow Dad and Uncle JT back out to the ring. My feet walk an inch above the ground as I am floating from the excitement of getting paid.

Chapter 8

As instructed, I follow Dad with Ambassador in hand and Uncle JT with Next To My Heart. As we walk, Dad begins talking about preparing these horses for the Fine Harness event.

"We will pretty much be doin' the same thing for these two horses… practicing, bathing, and brushing. The big difference is these two horses are competing in the Fine Harness," Dad explains.

In the Fine Harness event, a horse is attached to a four-wheeled carriage, which the rider sits in and controls the horse via long reins attached to the bit. The carriage, often constructed of a wooden flat bed adorned with a seat, would rest on four large but slender wheels. It would attach to the horse by two long posts that slid into a harness wrapped around the horse's body. The horse is then judged on its prancing perfection, similar to the gait categories, yet in pulling the carriage, the end result is timelessly different.

Over the years I have watched Dad numerous times practice a horse for this event. Not being on the horse and sharing that melded intimacy, I do not think he enjoyed it as much as the other categories, but he definitely took the same satisfaction in his work.

Having some understanding of the event I question, "Don't they perform two gaits? A walk and a trot?"

" I suppose that's right, but there is more to it than that," Dad replies with a smile.

I catch sight of Uncle JT shaking his head with a grin of his own adorning his face as Dad continues talking.

"Fine harness horses walk with a spring in their step... as light as air. They seem more graceful because speed is not a factor. Good show horses are beautiful, fine and alert. Now," he says as he brings Ambassador to the center of the ring and then climbs within the carriage, "Ambassador here is the oldest horse we brought with us. With just a few simple tugs on the reins and a few familiar sounds he will jump right into his routine."

With that, Dad tugs the reins to the left ever so slightly, while clicking his tongue, resonating a familiar sound into the air. Upon doing so, Ambassador reacts as he is supposed to and begins going through the motions of his technique.

After working Ambassador through the exercise, he navigates him over to Uncle JT and me, and exits the carriage. " What do you think?"

"That is some pretty neat stuff. He sure did look real pretty," I reply happily.

"That's what we're hoping for. He is a damn fine horse, yes sir he is," Dad says as he pats Ambassador on the side.

"You ready for Next To My Heart?" Uncle JT then asks.

"Always."

It only takes a few minutes to disconnect Ambassador from the carriage and then reattach it to Next To My Heart. Dad then begins to work Next To My Heart through the routine that Ambassador just performed, but her actions do not seem as natural. Dad has to work a bit harder to coerce the proper form from her and as such, she finishes much stronger than she starts. Pleased with the results, Dad brings her back over and the five of us return to the barn to cool down the horses.

After finishing and a bit ahead of schedule for the day, the three of us take our time enjoying the mood of the environment. With the radio now playing in the background, the music helps us catch our breath during a small break.

"You two want anything to drink?" Uncle JT then asks.

I look at Dad as he does the same to me and we both reply, "Sure!"

"Alright, I'm gonna go get us some pop from the stand. I'll be right back…"

"Sounds good," Dad replies.

As Uncle JT leaves, Dad walks over and turns the radio off, starts the record player and sits comfortably on a bench beside it. Then, slouching back he lowers his hat over his eyes and says kindly to me, "Enjoy the break son. Never know when you'll get another."

"Yes sir," I reply, as I walk over to him, picking up a piece of straw from a neighboring bushel. Then, mimicking him, I sit on the old wooden bench. My legs hang off it awkwardly, not quite touching the ground as his do, but I make the best of it anyway. I then place the straw into my mouth, close my eyes and enjoy the moment.

As I shut down my vision, my sense of smell seems to intensify. I never noticed it before, as it was so common it became as second nature as breathing air, but the scent of Absorbine hangs heavy in the air. The thick smell almost burns my nostrils and though I am use to it, in this quiet time its effects seem to be intensified. Luckily, the smell is a familiar one, because if not it would probably bring forth an onset of nausea and I wanted nothing of the sort. The scent of Absorbine is very particular, strong and thick. It is used to cool down horses and soothe muscle aches. In fact, Dad often used it on himself for the same reasons. So, needless to say around the barn and around the house, the scent has always been a familiar one.

Lost in my thoughts enjoying the break, I begin to hear a commotion across the way, outside our stable. Just then, Uncle JT comes in with frantic and heavy breath.

"Tom, you gotta come," he yells out quickly.

Upon hearing his words, Dad sits up worried and asks, "What's going on?"

"It's Sweet Mary. She's gone crazy wild! C'mon!"

On those words, Uncle JT takes off back out of the stable, with Dad following close behind. Eager to see what is going on, I spit out the thin stalk of straw from my mouth and follow them both.

Sweet Mary was a mare Dr. Bachtel had owned for five years and Dad had trained her during that time. Dad and the horse became close to each other, forming a bond similar to that he forges with all of his horses, one of mutual respect and admiration. Dad often said that Sweet Mary was one of the easiest horses to maintain and ride, but just as with some mares, she had a sensitive demeanor. She just needed a little extra time and a little extra care.

A few years ago, Dr. Bachtel decided to sell Sweet Mary. He had enough horses in his farm and because of the value of a show horse, he could turn a nice profit. Dad had tried to convince Dr. Bachtel not to sell her but was unsuccessful.

Uncle JT, Dad and I all rush to a nearby stable across the way to find Sweet Mary in the corner of the stall, sounding and acting wild and unruly. Dad looks at me and says softly, "Make sure you stay back boy," as he takes a step closer. Then louder, but in a gentle voice as not to further spook the horse he asks out, "What have you done to this mare?"

From off to the side, a man dressed in the common garb of horse trainer's jeans and a loose fitting button shirt, steps forward and says, "We did nothing." His face was unknown to me, but that is not too uncommon, as there are many trainers here who were not associated with Dad's crowd. These weekend events are often huge and have hundreds of horses competing in the different categories.

Though I did not know the man, Dad seems to as he responds to him, "Ken... nothing you say?"

"Nothing," the fairly well-built man replies again with a shrug of the shoulders and a sense of avoidance. "She just started losing control. I don't know what's wrong with her."

"Ain't nothing wrong with her," Dad replies with a sharp glance. He then shouts out, "JT, go and get Sam."

JT smiles and runs out of the stable and in less than three minutes, returns with the hi-fi and the Sam Cooke record. Dad rushes over to it, places the record on the turntable and then drops the needle down lightly to a specific song. There is a slight and quick scratch which presents the oncoming of music.

As the music begins and the song, *'You Were Made for Me'* starts to fill the stable, Dad sings along in accompaniment as he very slowly approaches Sweet Mary, occasionally whispering her name.

A fish was made to swim in the ocean, a boat was made to sail on the sea, sure as there are stars above, I know, I know, you were made for me.

"It's alright girl. C'mon Sweet Mary, there ain't nothin' wrong with ya. Listen, this is your favorite song."

As sure as there's a heaven up above me, from you I know I'll never be free, as sure there are stars above, I know, I know you were made for me.

"That's right girl, you're doin' just fine."

It is pure magic. Sweet Mary seems to calm the closer Dad nears and we all just watch in amazement. Then, he grabs her by the halter and clips on a leather reign which he uses to tranquilly lead her out of the stall.

As he walks her out, Dad looks over the body of the gentle horse and sees markings on her flanks from where she had been beaten and markings around her lower leg. You can see the sadness on his face, hidden behind the bags of anger surrounding his eyes. The horse is no longer his to train and as much as he would love to whip the man that had whipped this horse, he knows he would be finished if he did. So within earshot of everyone he says out to me, "Lee, let this be a lesson to you boy. Only a fool or a coward needs to harm a horse to get it to do what is needed. You remember that good. Do you hear me?"

I am afraid to really say anything. I know his anger is not directed at me, but it is still a situation I want to shy away from. As Dad and Sweet Mary exit the stable, a few of the men congratulate him on a feat well done. But I could tell this only made him uncomfortable. He only got to show his skill because of the pain and torment felt by Sweet Mary and he could not find consolation in that.

Chapter 9

By the time Dad finishes calming Sweet Mary and reluctantly returning her to her new owners, it is late afternoon. Our day's chores are finally starting to come to an end and my weary body is a bit thankful for that. As we return to the stalls, it dawns upon me we still have the last two horses to exercise before the weekend show.

Dell-ite and Painted Doll are both competing in the three gait. Horses competing in this division perform three gaits: the walk, trot, and canter both ways of the ring.

In the walk, the horse is alternately supported by three legs, and two legs, which are shifting in conjunction with every step. As humans move their arms to balance when walking and running, so too, the horse must move its head and neck to maintain its balance.

In the trot, the horse moves its legs in diagonal pairs. From the standpoint of the balance of the horse, this is a very stable gait and the horse need not make major balancing motions with its head and neck. Such movements, actually, can hurt a horse's final score.

In the canter, one of the horse's rear legs impels the horse forward. During this beat, the horse is supported only on that single leg while the remaining three legs are moving forward. On the next beat the horse catches itself on a rear and front legs while the other hind leg is still momentarily in contact with the ground. On the third beat the horse catches itself on the opposite front leg while the diagonal pair is momentarily still in contact with the ground.

Unique to this gait, listening to a horse canter, one can in most cases hear the three stages of this movement as though a drum had been struck three times in succession. Then there is a rest and immediately afterwards the three-beat occurs again.

Following the same course of action as we did with the other four horses, after Dad and Uncle JT have mounted the horses' bridles, we make our way to the training ring.

As we are waiting for an opening, Dad begins to check the equipment on the horses. First starting with the horseshoes and saddle, and then adjusting their bridles. As he does so, he calls me over to him.

"What is it Dad?" I ask as I come closer.

"Well, we have a few minutes before the ring opens," he replies as he glances out to the large training area. "So I thought I'd ask you how you're liking it here. What you expected?"

"Well, I did think there would be a little more excitement. A lot of it is like home so far."

"Once the competitions start tomorrow things will liven' up. But today's practices are just as important."

"I know, I know," I say whole heartedly. "It's great to see you and the others work with the horses," I then add.

Dad beams at me and not because of the compliment, but

instead as if I am missing an inner secret. "Well," he then says to me, "The truth is, as good as any of us are, we don't hold a candle to Tom Bass."

"Who's that? I heard you mention him before..." I ask, as at the time I am not familiar with the intimate details surrounding the history of the horseman.

"Tom Bass is a great forgotten horseman. For instance, he was the one who invented this special bit here to ease the pain that horses endure during training. But he never got any recognition for it."

"Really," I ask back in surprise.

"Absolute fact. Truth is, Tom Bass paved the way for people like me and JT. All us horsemen owe ourselves to good ole Tom Bass and that should never be forgotten... though it is to a lot of folks. Now, don't be wrong here son... it's very important. You shouldn't ever be envious of another man's accomplishments, but you sure as stone can be proud of them.

You see, for almost fifty years, Tom Bass trained thousands of horses to prance, bow, curtsy, dance, do the cakewalk and dozens of other tricks. But what's amazing is where he came from. He was born a slave in Missouri. He lived in Mexico, Missouri where he found work as a stable-hand. It was realized early on his skill with horses and he eventually became a trainer and established a reputation for trainin' even the most wild, violent horses. But he was able to do so with a calm voice and gentle touch."

"Kinda like you and Sweet Mary?" I ask.

"Somewhat. But he was much better than me or anyone else for that matter. Tom Bass was a true lover of horses and never beat horses and rarely raised his voice."

In wonderment at this man Dad so obviously admired, I want to know more. "So, did he stay in Mexico his entire life?"

"Mexico, Missouri?" Dad replies as he stands there, wiping his brow and adjusting his hat, "Naw. Bass moved to Kansas City where he trained and rode some of the world's most famous horses, including his prized Belle Beach. The word is, he not only loved that horse, but cared deeply about all the horses he trained. That's why he was an unbelievable horseman."

"Wow!" I exclaim.

"All true."

"Did you ever have a chance to meet him?"

"Naw, he was before my time. He trained thousands of horses in his time and we all use the techniques he mastered, but like him, we rarely get credit or recognition for our skills. That's a big reason why I don't ride these horses in the show. The great Tom Bass is widely ignored and that ain't right. If these white folk are gonna forget him, they sure as hell are gonna forget us, and men shouldn't be used like that. It ain't about the money or fame and it just ain't right to be used for all these other people. You should never compromise your soul for anything. That make sense to ya?"

"Yes sir," I reply, still in awe. It was hard to believe

everything my Dad loved and lived for... everything around us even, practically came from the work of one man. Additionally, a man I had never really heard much of before today.

Dad's story about Tom Bass always intrigued me and later in my college years I ended up devoting a great deal of time to learning more about him. Not only was Tom Bass the first known black horseman, but his accomplishments were staggering considering the era in which he lived.

In his career, he won competitions at every horse show in the country, earning more than 2,000 blue ribbons and winning championships at two World's Fairs. During his years in Kansas City, he was instrumental in the formation of Kansas City's first horse show, The American Royal, and for a long time he was the only black man to exhibit at this show. Also while in Kansas City, he trained horses for many of the city's wealthiest citizens including Loula Long, a famed horsewoman in her own right. Then in 1897, Tom Bass received an unprecedented invitation by Queen Victoria to attend London's Diamond Jubilee with his famous horse Miss Rex, but he declined her invitation because he feared traveling over the ocean.

Although he trained and rode many famous horses including Rex McDonald and Miss Rex, his favorite mare was Belle Beach. Today Tom Bass' grave marker in Mexico, Missouri displays a picture of him riding his beloved Belle.

Just then, my private thoughts are interrupted as Uncle JT says out, "Looks like it's our time Mojo."

"Alright, lets get this done then boys," Dad replies.

Over the next thirty minutes or so, Dad rides both Dell-ite and Painted Doll through their own practices. As with the other four horses before them, both respond in kind to Dad's touch and call, and work through their gaits without any problem.

As Dad is finishing up, Dr. Bachtel arrives at the training ring. Seeing him, Dad asks, "So how did things go up at the clubhouse Doc?"

"About the same as can be expected Tom," the doctor replies. "Same pretentiousness that happens at all these events."

"I can only imagine," Dad replies. So, you wanna give her a ride," he then adds, while patting Dell-ite.

"Sure. Might be good for me to get a little time with the horse before the big event."

On those words, Dad trots Dell-ite over to Dr. Bachtel and the two men switch positions. As Dr. Bachtel rides the horse though, it is apparent something is wrong. For the next five minutes we watch him control the horse and it is apparent Dell-ite does not respond well to his gestures.

Seeing this, Dad responds. "Doc. You gotta remember to relax with the horses. They will respond better to you if you do. Have patience with this horse and she'll have patience with you."

It is obvious that Dr. Bachtel listens to the words and in doing so, his ride seems to improve during the final moments. As he then stops to dismount, Dr. Bachtel says, "I'm telling you

Tom, these horses only listen to you."

"No sir. Just stay calm with them and you'll do just fine."

Upon completion of the workouts, Uncle JT and I lead the two horses back to the stable, while Dad and Dr. Bachtel engage in conversation up ahead of us. As we enter the barn area, Dad grabs the reins of Painted Doll and leads her to her stall.

Seeing the beautiful horse, Dr. Bachtel walks over. Then, rubbing Painted Doll's face gently he says out, "This sure is a beautiful horse, ain't it Tom?"

Dad does not offer a verbal response, but does shoot a friendly and revealing smile toward Dr. Bachtel.

Laughing, Dr. Bachtel then adds, "Sure is amazing what this horse has been through…"

And with those words, Dr. Bachtel begins to recount the story of the Painted Doll. A story he and my dad remember so well.

Chapter 10

"I remember it like it was yesterday," Dr. Bachtel says as he begins his story. "In the early 50's, I purchased a horse named Silver Rocket from a ranch in Kentucky. Silver Rocket wasn't a bad horse and with Tom's training, she really blossomed. We put her in competitions as a dappled-gray junior horse and she won some nice junior harness shows. Her unique look really struck a cord with the judges and after Tom here was able to spend some time with her, Silver's form really came into place too."

"That's right," Dad adds in. "She sure was a good horse. Mild-tempered for sure."

Dr. Bachtel smiles and then continues on, "Unfortunately, her good graces were not to last. You see, once her dappled color began to fade, the horse stopped winning shows."

"That bird sure don't hunt no more did it Mojo?" Uncle JT asks as he also listens on.

"Yeah," Dad replies, "She really lost her luster in the judges' eyes. She was just like any other trained horse..."

"Well-trained horse," Uncle JT interrupts.

"Yeah, just like any other well-trained horse," Dad smiles. "Once her dapples faded, she lost the uniqueness which was winning her all those competitions."

"But isn't that unfair?" I ask with my youthful innocence,

motioning to Uncle JT as I finish, "I mean, what horse can hunt birds?"

The men collectively laugh at my comment. I had heard this story before, but never were birds mentioned. I learned later on that among the horsemen, the comment, 'that bird don't hunt' simply means the horse no longer showed promise and was a loser.

Continuing with a chuckling undertone, Dr. Bachtel then adds, "The problem was not in the horse's skill or training, no sir. The horse's pigment had grown to be so close to white in color and with the rails at the shows being white as well, the judges could not clearly distinguish the horse's finite movements. So needless to say, Silver Rocket would literally just blend into the background and for all the grace in her performances, she just could not win.

The situation really haunted me. She is a damn good horse and had proven it with her victories. Something had to be done. So, one evening I was talking with the missus about the entire situation. As you all know," the doctor turns and says to Uncle JT, "Mrs. B. is quite the accomplished rider in her own right."

"Yes sir she is. Without a doubt."

"She always has been a big part in the Dells and that evening as we were talking about Silver Rocket, she had a fantastic idea. Why not dye the horse?"

Uncle JT then asks, "I have to know. What made her think of that idea? I ain't ever heard of it before Painted Doll here."

" To be honest with you, I was just as surprised at her suggestion at first. But then she related it to women dying their hair. If they can do it to look their best, why not a horse? So, that evening we decided to dye Silver Rocket a deep chestnut brown. And boy can I tell you, Tom here was not at all happy with that."

"How come Tom?" Uncle JT asks.

"It really is unfair to the horse. And, I especially thought so back then. After all, if that was her God-given color and nature decided to fade her color out, then who were we to alter the course of nature and God?"

Happy with the memory, Dr. Bachtel then continues on, "In recourse, I explained it to Tom how Eileen explained it to me… about how women would dye their hair to look their best."

"I still didn't like it though. Still now I ain't too sure 'bout it."

"That's true, he did keep to his protest, but for me an investment is an investment and Silver Rocket still had many good years ahead of her. So, we went ahead and dyed her out."

"That very next day," Dad adds.

"That's right. That next day we brought her out of the stall and into an open field. Tom and I filled a bunch of buckets with water and dye, and rubbed it into her coat real nice. The whole process took a couple hours as we wanted to make sure she looked even."

"If I was gonna be forced to do it," Dad adds, "I figured we might as well do it right."

" After we finished the second coat," Dr Bachtel continues, "Silver Rocket was now a chestnut brown horse who we renamed Painted Doll. And I must say, the decision was a good one. Right Tom?"

"As much as I hate to admit it, Mrs. B. sure was right. Painted Doll looked like a natural beauty…"

"And it resurrected her career. She went on to win competition after competition. In fact, just a couple years ago, a national horse magazine even wrote about her and I've been keeping this in my pocket ever since."

Dr. Bachtel reaches inside his sport coat and pulls out a tattered piece of paper from which he reads, "… *The Painted Doll, this mare is a nationally recognized phenomenon of our time and is a 'first' in the horse show world. Her transformation into a flashily marked bright chestnut with white `blaze and socks accomplished via a tinting, dispelled the color-jinx which had hovered over her. Her undisputed victory in the highly competitive three gaited championship, winner of the over- two division at Waynesburg and also the over-two stakes at Moundsville is a testament to the success of her rebirth.*"

Additionally, another publication actually said that, "*as the new Painted Doll tested and tried at seven of inter-state major events and emerged champion at five of them, she rightfully wears the crown denoting supremacy.*"

"So she went from a horse that couldn't win… to a horse

that couldn't lose," Uncle JT adds.

"Pretty much," Dr. Bachtel replies. "Pretty much…"

"See Lee," Dad says to me as he turns in my direction, "for some people, color is everything and if you ever don't believe that, just remember Painted Doll here."

Chapter 11

Later that evening, as dusk's presence makes its way over the fairgrounds, our work is done for the day. By far, today was the day where everyone has been challenged with the intensity of a burdening long day of work. Not just in our stable, but across the fairgrounds and for all the competitors, today was all about prepping the horses. With today's work and the trainers cultivating their magic long ago, the stage is set for the owners and it is their opportunity to shine tomorrow. Today however, with the training, cleaning and pampering of the horses, was where a good stable crew could really make a difference. Competition time was for the trainers, owners, and horses, but this evening was for everyone who helped make this weekend possible.

" How did the day go for you?" Dad asks me from across the room.

Sitting on a bail of hay with my back arched comfortably, resting against our tack wall, I reply happily, "I had some fun and I think I did pretty good too."

Laughing, Dad replies, "Well, you sure did. You sure did. I think tomorrow is gonna go real well."

"So do I," Uncle JT adds, releasing his words over his shoulder as he places the equipment back on the tack wall.

"What's left?" I ask, wanting to know if there is anything

more that needs to be done.

"Not much really," Dad responds. "JT and I are gonna run through all the equipment making sure it is ready for tomorrow and then we'll get some food at the concession stand. You're pretty much done."

The words are bittersweet to hear. Admittedly I am thankful to know my duties for the day are done. Today was a lot more work than I expected. On the other hand, I feel a large sense of contentment in being able to help, especially because of the connection I felt I made with the horses.

Still resting on the bail of hay, I watch Dad surveying the last horse for the evening. A gentle wind blows through the stable softly and my eyelids get heavy. The soft breeze lulls me more into a passive reflection and without realizing it, I soon find myself drifting off to sleep.

After only a few minutes of welcome slumber, I feel a nudge against my shoulder forcing me out of my nap. Dad is standing over me and looking at me he asks, "Everything ok son? You tired?"

Rubbing my eyes, I stand up off the bail and respond, "All's good Dad. Sorry about that."

"It's nothing. I just thought you might be hungry. Let's get something to eat."

"I sure am," I reply as I look back.

"Let's go JT. We can finish up afterwards. Let's get to gettin' while the gettins' still hot."

"I hear ya there," Uncle JT responds, and with that the three of us head outside the stable and join up with the other horsemen.

"Anyone hear how Willie Mays did today?" Eddie Stivers asks as we enter the eating area.

"Yeah," Uncle Bill responds from the table covered in burgers and fries, "Two for four with a double, run scored and an RBI."

"I take it the Giants won then?"

"Sure did, 5-1."

"Man, that Willie Mays is the best to ever play. Believe me," Bulgia chimes in, already half done with his own meal.

"I don't know," Uncle JT interjects. "Is he really better than Jackie Robinson was?"

All the men break out into a collective exhale. The question is one which has been posed many times before to people in all walks of life and just adds relevance to the regular nature of these horsemen.

"Willie can do it all," Bulgia replies. "Hell, the man can run as good as he can hit and field better than anyone in the league."

"Man," Eddie Stivers retorts, "If not for Jackie, Willie wouldn't even be in the league."

Most of the crowd agrees with the statement, except for Pretty Boy who says, "I don't know about that."

Bulgia looks over and asks, "What are you talking about? I

mean. I love Willie and all, but Jackie broke the barriers man."

"So you mean to tell me if not for Jackie Robinson," Pretty Boy retorts, "there would never have been a 'first' Negro baseball player? Hell, it was bound to be someone. If not Jackie, it would'a been Satchel, Josh Gibson, or eventually a Willie Mays. There is too much money in baseball and too much talent for the white owners to ignore."

"You know," Uncle Bill says, "I think for once I might actually agree with Pretty Boy. If it wasn't gonna be Jackie it woulda been someone else sooner or later."

"Damn straight," Pretty Boy adds. "If Willie was ten, twenty years older, Negroes woulda been in baseball that much earlier. I mean Jackie was good and all, but Willie, he is a whole 'nother level."

"Man Bill," Bulgia says. "What's going on? I think I'm agreeing with Pretty Boy here today too…"

"I wouldn't worry about it too much," Uncle Bill replies, "the Cubs dropped another today. All is still right in the world."

The men laugh as Bulgia then says, "I never knew you were such a Mays fan Pretty Boy."

"I'm not really," he replies. "But I see a lot of similarities between me and him."

More sighs than laughter erupt around the eating area at that comment. Begging to know, Dad chimes in and asks, "How exactly are you like Willie Mays, Pretty Boy?"

"Well, it's simple. Willie Mays is the best. He's taken

baseball to a whole other level. I'm kinda like that. I'm taken these competitions to a whole 'nother level."

Even I can't contain my laughter at Pretty Boy's comments and as I shovel in bites of dinner between my exhales of glee, I listen to Bulgia say, "Man, that's sacrilegious. You can't compare yourself to Willie Mays."

"Think about it," Pretty Boy replies, "Willie is a 5-tool player... I'm a 5-tool trainer. Hell, I help pick the horses to buy, I train 'em, and I ride 'em. I do it all. There ain't no one like me... 'specially no Negro."

"Whoa now," Uncle Bill adds, "Them are some big statements your makin'."

"Also, wouldn't that make you more like Jackie Robinson? You're riding in a white man's world after all," Uncle JT asks.

"Naw. Tom Bass was our Jackie Robinson. I'll give him his credit there. But I guarantee if I was born earlier, it would be Pete Jones you all would be talking about."

On those words, just about everyone sitting around the eating area throws the remainder of their bread rolls at Pretty Boy, releasing a plethora of catcalls at the same time.

"Man," Bulgia then says, "You ain't no Willie Mays, Jackie Robinson or Tom Bass. Hell, you ain't even the best one here."

Pretty Boy replies, "Are we gonna go there again?"

"Boy, you're the only one here that plays the fool for the owners," Uncle Bill states.

"Plays the fool?" Pretty Boy yells out with an undertone of

anger. "The only fool here is you!"

"Calm yourself down Pete. Outside of this circle, who else at these fairgrounds will know of Tom Bass? And like Jackie Robinson," he adds with a friendly grin, "Tom Bass was the best there's ever been. If these white folk don't remember him, how the hell they ever gonna remember you? I guarantee in fifty years the world will know all about Jackie Robinson and Willie Mays. But Tom Bass and Pete Jones, those men will just be memories our kids share with their kids... kinda like Lee over there. Ain't no one else gonna give a damn 'bout us... or you."

"Like I've always said," Bulgia adds with a whisper as he shakes his head as he did the night before, "We're just a few pieces of chocolate chips in a bucket of buttermilk. Don't you ever forget that."

"Man, that's the problem with you all. You need to think different... think big, man! People will remember Pete 'Pretty Boy' Jones for sure, I guarantee it."

On those words, Pretty Boy stands in a huff and exits the eating area, making his way back to his stable. Never one to want to exclude anyone, even Pretty Boy, Dad stands to go after him. As he does though, Uncle Bill grabs his shoulder and says, "Let him go Tom. We know any man who thinks he is as good as Willie Mays has some problems to work out."

Dad laughs at the comment, shakes his head and sits back down. For a few minutes, the eating area is silent, save for the crackling of a large fire coming from the pit in the center. The flames dance to the silent sounds of a now lapsed day, hidden beneath the veil of evening's darkness. Each man is lost within the vision and lost within their own thoughts. Each one silently hopes that Pretty Boy is right and that he would be remembered... that any of them would be remembered. But also each to a man, they all know such dreams are beyond even childhood fantasies and for the first time, in that moment of silence, I understood the pride they have for their work.

For these men it was not about fame and fortune, though none of them would have turned it down. It was about the honor and history of their trade. It was about being the best horseman you could be while maintaining your dignity. It was about taking on difficult obstacles of life and making the best of it, even when prejudices engulfed you everyday. If not for Tom Bass, who pioneered horse training for them and was certainly the Jackie Robinson of the saddle horse world, these competitions would be different. Their lives would be different.

Chapter 12

Saturday

Saturday morning comes as early as Friday's did, but with it follows a heightened level of excitement. All the work these trainers have put into the horses comes down to these last two days of the weekend and for all the friendly bantering back and forth, they each want to win.

In these competitions, winning is of course the most prominent end goal, but second to that is simply placing. *Play to place*, as the old saying goes. Owners of course love the bragging rights associated with a first place victory, but the money, press and prestige is still bountiful for second through fifth place as well. A fifth place victory pays for the entry fee, plus a bit more. A sixth place finish or not even making it past the first day simply turns the entire event into a bit of disappointment.

Placing also puts your stable club, the horses and most importantly the owner, in the press articles that cover the events. Overall, the trainers who stay on the longest are those whose horses continually place and often times, it must be done in spite of the owner's own riding abilities. A challenge to say the least, but one each of these trainers is ready for.

"Son," Dad says as I rise from the cot, "Today is the day. We have the qualifying rounds today. The three gait in the morning, the fine harness in the afternoon and the five this evening. If today goes well, perhaps we will also do well tomorrow."

After thinking about it for a moment, Uncle JT adds from across the room, "Hell, as much as Bachtel wants to do well in the gait, if today doesn't go well, tomorrow won't matter that much either."

Laughing, Dad responds as he walks over to the edge of the stable rows, "You're probably right there JT. But King Cloud won't let us down, will you boy."

As if understanding exactly what my dad is saying, the large horse bounces his head in affirmation. Dad then adds as he rubs King's snout and as Uncle JT grabs a couple pails, "Yeah, I like our chances today. Now Lee, we need these horses good and watered. You want to impress your Momma tomorrow with all your hard work right?"

"Yes sir," I respond quietly.

" The best way for us to do that is to bring these horses home with a ribbon. And that all starts right now. Let's make sure they are good and hydrated. Its gonna be hot today."

I pick up the pails and rush out to the spigot as Dad and Uncle JT lay out some oats and straw for the horses. Today is going to be a good day… we can all feel it.

After the morning feed and watering is done, Dad, Uncle JT and I meet with the others around the eating area for some hotcakes and coffee. The morning sun seems to have gotten a jump-start on the day and the brilliant hues of orange filling the darkened sky are invigorating.

As we all eat, the chatter stays specific to the competitions and primarily on the day's big events. On that topic, Pretty Boy speaks up as he sips a cup of coffee, "So, any of you ready to just go on and give up now?"

"That depends Pete," Uncle Bill says from his seat on one of the logs backed against an exterior barn wall, "We'll concede if you do it first. I promise we will," he then adds with an amicable glance.

Looking over, Pretty Boy responds, "Hell Bill, it ain't you I'm worried about. Who you got going today?"

" We're feeling real good about Kentucky Sunrise…"

"That horse still alive?" Pretty Boy goads on, "Hell, didn't Tom Bass himself train her first?"

"What, you mean you can't remember for sure who Bass trained?" one of the Stivers brothers yells out in reference to last night's conversation.

Pretty Boy turns his head and retorts, "I don't know why you're even talking Eddie. When was the last time you even placed in a gait?"

"Seeing as how we usually don't even enter the gaits, I can say for fact it's been awhile…"

"Well then…" Pretty Boy says with a sense of assertion followed by a wide smile.

"So who you got going today then?" Bulgia asks aloud.

"In the three we are running Golden Honey and Holiday Dream. In the five it'll be Earl Gray and October Star."

"All fine horses," Dad chimes in.

"See, Tom here understands…"

"Too bad you'll be riding them," Uncle JT then adds.

The group erupts once more into familiar laughter. From an outsider's perspective, it may seem as if Pretty Boy takes a lot of ribbing from the group, but it is a role he revels in. He is as much a part of this horsemen fraternity as any of these men and for all his bravado, to a man, they all love his fire. He is the counterweight in the group and one none of them would ever wish away.

Shaking off the half-handed insult as if it means nothing, Pretty Boy then asks my dad, "So who you running today?"

"The Doc is riding Dell-ite and Mrs. B is riding Painted Doll in the three…"

"That Painted Doll is a tough horse to beat. She's been around the block a few times," Pretty Boy interrupts.

Continuing on, Dad adds, "In the five we got King Cloud and Hot Toddy."

"My money is on King," a voice bellows out.

"Hell, my money is on King," Pretty Boy laughs out. "That's a damn fine horse. But we ain't given' it to ya that easy."

"I would never expect ya to Pete," Dad replies. After finishing his cup of coffee, he tosses it out and motions to me while saying out, "Alright everyone. We have a lot to do before the hat drops. Good luck to everyone."

"You too Tom," Uncle Bill says back, as do all the men in the group. With a wave, Dad, Uncle JT and I exit the eating area and return back to the stable.

As we walk under our welcoming tack banner, the morning day excitement and anticipation is in full swing. This morning, the routine grooming of the horses takes on an extra meaning, after all it is show day!

We start with the two horses that are showing in the first competition, the three gait. We keep their routine the same as every other average morning for sake of retaining normality, but we did mix in a little extra pampering.

As Dad is looking over the day's competition chart, he sees that Dell-ite is showing soon, so we start with her. She is the most beautiful dark, smoky black horse and has a fun, engaging personality. She loves to eat apples and before each ride or workout, Dad always gives her a couple of apples.

On this day, he lets me feed the apples to Dell-ite. As he stands and cuts the apples with his pocketknife, deftly maneuvering the blade through the meat of the apple by pressing on the blade with his thumb, he hands me the large pieces. He reminds me to make sure to keep my hand flat and bridged-up so Dell-ite can easily swallow-up the apples without swallowing-up my fingers.

I have always been a little nervous feeding apples to the

horses for fear of losing a few fingers, but I want to be brave standing before Dad and Uncle JT. It's a strange feeling when a horse eats from your hand. When Dell-ite reaches down to engulf the cut-up apples, her lips just nuzzle gently against my hand as if to ensure not to harm me.

As Dell-ite nibbles at the apple in my hand, Uncle JT walks over to me and quickly sticks out his right hand where three fingers are heavily wrapped in gauze and band-aids. My eyes grow large as I stare at his hand. He then shouts, "This is what happened the last time I fed this damn horse some apples."

Upon hearing Uncle JT's declaration, I hastily pull my hand back. Doing so causes Uncle JT and Dad to burst out into laughter and I quickly realize I was on the butt end of another one of their jokes. For a moment I understand how Pretty Boy feels and it only makes me love the fact I am included among these men I idolize.

Chapter 13

"Let's get going," Dad says to Uncle JT, as he grabs the reins of Painted Doll.

We had just finished preparing Painted Doll with her 'show time' grooming that consists of therapeutic brushing, the laying down of the saddlecloth and placing the saddle upon her. We are eager to get the day's competitions started. Dad and Uncle JT completed the preparation by applying the halter, bit and reins to the horse. In the end, Painted Doll looks majestically groomed and polished in the burgundy and gold colors representing the Dells.

The three gait starts at 9:00am, and I am surprised to find there are a large number of horses competing in the event. The entrant horses for each event are split into four classes and of all those, twelve will make it to the final money round.

Earlier in the day at breakfast, Uncle JT had told me how the larger stables would enter two horses in each competition to increase their chances of making it to the money round the next day. In this three gait event, we are entering both Painted Doll and Dell-ite.

Although the championship rounds of the competitions are not until tomorrow, the excitement is electrifying even for these qualifying rounds. The fairgrounds are full today with fanatic followers who have admission to every event via an all access type pass. Moment by moment, the excitement and electricity swells across the fairgrounds.

Approaching the ring area, my jaw drops. In the two days I have been here, I had not yet toured the entire fairgrounds. Instead, my time has been spent by Dad's side.

In the fairgrounds, there is one main ring with a grandstand that casts a long morning shadow over the ring. Beyond that are two other rings, if they could be called such a thing. These practice rings are mainly just large dirt circles, used to warm up and exercise the horses. From an aerial view, it would seem as if the rings were stacked like a triangle.

The grandstand, large and obvious, stands in front of the main ring. Even this early in the morning for the first qualifying events, the bleachers are about two-thirds full.

Moving toward one of the outer rings, I see both Dr. and Mrs. Bachtel standing there, awaiting our arrival. Dr. Bachtel is wearing a dapper, finely tailored chocolate brown colored suit with flecks of a softer, more subtle tan peppered throughout it. It has a slightly tapered fit with double vents in the back and two buttons. His trousers are double pleated, with the bottoms slightly above his black riding boots. Attached to his shining black boots are sparkling silver spurs. On his head rests a matching fedora hat, tilted slightly to the left and from his mouth hangs a burning cigarette.

Standing by his side, Mrs. Bachtel, a petite woman with pinned-up auburn hair, looks stunning. She is in a black and white houndstooth check top and the sleeveless piece has a bold white collar, two front pockets and a front tabbed tie. Her waist high black jacket is accented with a black tie scarf. She nudges Dr. Bachtel in the side as we arrive and a smile beams radiant from her face, echoing her raw enthusiasm.

" Fellas how are things looking this morning?" Dr. Bachtel asks as we move toward him.

"Looking good Doc. Painted Doll here is all ready to go," Dad replies. Then, turning to Mrs. Bachtel he tips his own hat and issues a greeting, "Mrs. B…"

"Hello Thomas," she replies as she walks toward Painted Doll. Mrs. Bachtel's comfort level with the horses is obvious. An accomplished rider in her own right, it is very rare she would ever miss the opportunity to ride Painted Doll, the horse she is going to take through the three gait today. They have always been very close, even before Mrs. Bachtel suggested the idea of dying Painted Doll the chestnut brown.

Turning back to Doc, Dad then continues, "how ya feeling Doc? You ready?"

"I sure am Tom, but I think Eileen is a bit more nervous than me. She has to go first," Dr Bachtel replies as he looks around. "Some sharp competition today."

"Won't lie to you, it sure is. In addition to Pete Jones over there, you got Southern Belle from Hickory Creek Stables, Prince Victor from Cherry Hill Farms, and a few others who have made some noise on the circuit. We'll be looking good just to make it to tomorrow. Unfortunately with this much talent, its anyone's game."

"Any advice for me and the missus?"

"Just go out there and do your best. The horses will take care of you both. They know what they are doing."

"That's right honey," Mrs. Bachtel interjects, "I know Painted Doll will do her best." Then, nuzzling her nose into Painted Doll's she whispers, "Won't you Doll?"

Just then, a bell rings from the side. "Honey," Dr. Bachtel says, "Time for you to give them hell."

"That's what we're going to do!" Mrs. Bachtel replies with a confident look.

On those words, Dad stands next to Mrs. Bachtel's left leg and faces Painted Doll's rear. Reaching down, he grips the lower part of Mrs. Bachtel's leg right above the ankle with both hands. He then crouches slightly, smartly using his thighs instead of his back to lift her. On the count of three, Dad begins to straighten himself, bouncing Mrs. Bachtel up as he does. Mrs. Bachtel then twists herself around a bit and climbs on top of the horse. Afterwards, Dad, Uncle JT and I move to an area adjacent to the ring to watch the event, as Dr. Bachtel moves to the grandstand area.

"You enjoying yourself?" Uncle JT asks me as we lean against the railing.

"I'm having a great time," I reply as I stand on the edge of the lower railing to get my shorter head into viewing position.

Looking at all the people, I cannot believe the fanfare associated with Dad's job. He trains the horses that entertain everyone. Dad and the rest of the horsemen are all like the head coaches of their own football teams and on any given weekend, it is up to the stable team to come through. " What exactly is going on here?" I ask as I point out to the horses in the ring.

"Well," Dad replies, "the concept of these competitions comes from an old English style of riding known as..."

"Dressage I think the proper folk call it," Uncle JT adds after Dad ponders the word for a few long seconds.

"That's right, dressage. Anyways, it's a type of riding that shows a horse's ability during show time, kinda like in the three gait here. Many types of horses are allowed to compete, but some are bred better than others at it. These horses generally stand 15-16 hands and weigh between 1000-2000 pounds. Even as big as they are, a good show horse will simply dance and prance to the commands of their riders with ease. It is pretty amazing. They are judged on a series of movements and high animated actions while rounding the show rings."

"How do you think they will do?"

" As I told Doc," Dad replies, "The competition is stiff today. We always shoot for first place, but this Canfield show is a big one with a lot of great horses. I think making it to the money round tomorrow will be a feat in itself and should be considered a success."

"That's for sure," Uncle JT adds. Southern Belle there is outta Lexington, and I hear she is a damn good horse."

" We're gonna get to see," Dad retorts as he motions to the ring on the other side of the railing.

With that, we all turn our heads and press our bodies against the outer railing, the place where most of the crew and stable trainers watch the happenings of the show.

As the horses prepare to make their way into the ring, the ringmaster, a tall white man in a finely pressed black suit and slicked back, dark hair, speaks into a microphone and speakers assembled in front of the grandstand.

"Ladies and Gentlemen, welcome to the Qualifying round of the Three-Gait Amateur Circuit here at the Canfield Horse Show. We have an exciting show for you today. We have four classes of horses competing with nearly fifty entrants. Each class will have three horses move on to tomorrow's final championship round where the top five horses of the remaining twelve will be selected as winners. If the entrants are ready, let us begin!"

The crowd releases a calm and controlled clap and I follow suit when Dad and Uncle JT do the same.

The announcer introduces the horses from the first class of which Painted Doll is a participant, as is Pretty Boy on Golden Honey and they each enter the ring in single file. As they are doing so, I watch the judges and am interested in their jobs. They are wearing dark suits and fedora hats, observing the horses and riders with close scrutiny.

As the horses and their riders enter the ring, trotting in slow with animated high steps, we watch with confidence. The horses are separated from each other by a full-bodied length.

Once everyone is in, the commands to the riders are issued out from the ringmaster first to walk the horses, then trot and finally finish through with the canter. It takes nearly fifteen minutes for the horses to go through the entire technique and while they are doing so, the judges walk around the infield observing and judging the movements of both the riders and the horses.

After they finish, the riders are commanded to move the horses to the grassy infield for the line-up.

As this is going on, Dad turns and mentions to Uncle JT, "Look at them go. Mrs. B sure is having a great ride."

"She sure is!" he replies.

Painted Doll and Golden Honey are separated by seven horses, with Mrs. Bachtel and Painted Doll near the front of the line. The horses then line up in a perfectly uniform horizontal line with roughly three feet between each horse on the grassy infield. The three judges then move toward the line of horses with clipboard and pen in hand. As each judge approaches each individual horse, the rider places the reins in his left hand and removes his hat with his right and bows to the judge. During the entire motion, the horse remains in a perfect halt and salute position. A good halt and salute can put both a rider and his horse in a good light with the judges and can influence winning or losing.

Watching Mrs. Bachtel intently, the judges next ask her to move Painted Doll three steps back, as they do with the rest of the riders. She does so and I see one of the judges scribble a few markings onto the piece of paper resting on his clipboard. While they are going through this motion, I notice Dad makes his way to the gate. At first I am unsure why, but soon see him enter the ring along with the other trainers to help the riders remove the saddles.

"What are they doing?" I ask Uncle JT.

" It's called conformation. The judges are checking the form. They are checking for things like how eye-catching the horse's shoulders are, how strong and level the back is, the muscled legs and so on."

"Wow, I had no idea it was this detailed."

"Pretty amazing ain't it…"

"Sure is," I whisper back, engrossed by the sight before me. After the judges are finished inspecting Painted Doll, Mrs. Bachtel is told to mount up once more. On that note, Dad refastens the saddle to Painted Doll and then gives Mrs. Bachtel a leg-up back on the horse.

I am quite surprised by the complexity of how the qualifiers for tomorrow's championship round are chosen. The entire process is very formal and the outcome rests completely on the judges' shoulders. As the judges are deciding, I notice that Mrs.

Bachtel is one of two women in the competition and I wonder how it makes her feel, or if she thinks anything of it at all.

Just then, I see movement from the judges as they hand a slip of paper to the ringmaster. After taking a moment to read it to himself, he folds it up and says, "Alright folks... I will need these three horses to move forward and receive your ribbon. You have qualified for tomorrow's final championship show."

The crowd becomes silent as does the breathing of Uncle JT beside me. I see his fingers clenched tightly, interwoven together like a knot.

"Southern Belle, ridden by Mr. Ashley Turnbull of Hickory Creek Farms from Lexington, Kentucky," is the first name spoken out by the ringmaster. The jet black horse trots slowly forward, a surprise to no one. As he steps forward, one of the judges approaches him and hands him a long red preliminary winning ribbon.

While Southern Belle is receiving her ribbon, the ringmaster continues on, "Next we have Tequila Sunrise, ridden by Mr. Stephen Jackson of Apple Farms from Chase City, Virginia, please come forward."

"Not surprising," Uncle JT whispers to me without looking in my direction. "That horse is real unique with great technique too. You'd think that coat ain't natural, but it is," he adds, referring to the horse's off-white tone, which in the sun reflects back a somewhat rusty beige tone.

As Tequila Sunrise receives his ribbon, the announcer then calls out the final name for this qualifying class, "And next we have Painted Doll, ridden by Mrs. Eileen Bachtel of The Dells Farm from North Canton, Ohio."

We cheer in excitement as Mrs. Bachtel brings Painted Doll forward to receive her ribbon.

"There you have it folks, our three finalists from this round. Now let's hear it for all our competitors."

As the event ends, everyone in the stands begins to clap one more time as Uncle JT nudges me. "C'mon," he says.

Uncle JT and I follow back alongside the railing to meet the horses, the riders, Dad and Dr. Bachtel who had started to make his way back near the gate when the qualifiers were announced. As we walk up, I hear the tail end of the conversation between the two Bachtel's.

"Don't get too used to it. Hopefully you won't be the only Dells Farm qualifying today," Dr. Bachtel says to his wife with a wide smile.

"Are you kidding? Painted Doll and I have been used to winning for years," she replies back.

As the two laugh, Dad grabs Painted Doll's reins and says to Mrs. Bachtel, "Good work out there."

"Definitely not bad. I don't know that we were necessarily any better than the others, all the horses were real good. But I'm glad it went our way."

As the second class of entrants begins to enter the ring, Dad turns to Dr. Bachtel and says, " we're going to take Painted Doll back to the barn and get her cooled down. We'll be back shortly with Dell-ite. You're in the fourth class right?"

"That's right Tom. Hurry back when you can."

"Don't worry, we'll be here."

Without wasting any more time, we bring Painted Doll back to the barn. While Uncle JT and I are cooling her down, Dad starts prepping Dell-ite by applying her equipment.

About thirty minutes later, we arrive back at the ring and the third class is just finishing up. While Dad gives a few final words of encouragement to Dr. Bachtel, Uncle JT and I head back to the side area so we can watch the final class.

During the routine, Dell-ite looks sharp and crisp, but unfortunately, so do a few of the other horses. Dell-ite is definitely top five material in our eyes, but regrettably, only three can move on to tomorrow's final event.

Unfortunately, after the horses run through their routines, the qualifiers are announced and Dell-ite is not among them. I suspected Dr. Bachtel to be angry, but in contrast, he was actually quite pleased. The horse showed well and Dr. Bachtel rode Dell-ite with a certain grace. It was obvious the few minutes he spent working with Dad yesterday were helpful. Disappointingly, it was just not meant to be.

Chapter 14

Over the next couple of hours, we finished cooling down Dell-ite, prepared Ambassador for his event and even found a little time to relax for a few minutes. I had no idea how fast-paced competition day would be, but with our success in the three gait, I found myself eager to continue on. During our short break, I was paying attention to the horses while in conversation with Dad and Uncle JT.

With about fifteen minutes to go before the start of the Fine Harness event, Dr. Bachtel joins us at the tack as we finish the preparation with Ambassador and ushers out, "We only have ten minutes to get this horse strapped in, so lets put a move on it."

"Do you need me to do anything?" I ask Dad, wanting to help.

"Just follow behind us and help us make sure all the buckles are fastened as they should be. We don't want the cart coming loose during the competition."

It takes us under ten minutes for Ambassador to be strapped in. The Jerald Horse, Royal Classic Buggy we are using is the best in the industry. A polished buggy is as important as a polished horse and the darkened steel on this carriage shines in the early afternoon sun. Sleek and impressive in the show ring, the Jerald Royal Classic has a body of seasoned wood polished to a shine surpassed only by the chrome parts and wheels. The luxurious velvet cushion is regal and coordinates with the colors of our stable, burgundy and gold.

As in the three gait, Dad, Uncle JT and I take our positions with the rest of the staff for the event as Dr. Bachtel climbs into Ambassador's carriage. While all the contestants in the first stage are entering the ring to the ringmaster's voice, I ask Dad, "So, how did the fine harness come about? I mean, it's the only one that uses extra equipment. How did something like that come to be?"

" I think this event comes from a long time ago. But whatever the reason, the real beauty lies in performance of the horse. To win in this event, not only does the horse have to be graceful, but he has to have the strength and poise to do it while pulling a carriage."

"That's gotta be tough…"

"It sure is. I'm not a big fan of the event, but it serves its purpose I suppose."

"Why don't you like it?" I ask.

"It's not that I don't like it. I just prefer more of the natural beauty behind the other categories."

"That reminds me. I don't think I ever asked. Why exactly did you start training horses. I mean, I know you love 'em and all…"

"That I do," Dad replies to me. "But that ain't all of it. As you know, your grandfather taught me how to ride horses. Back then we had little choices of jobs as Negroes in Kentucky.

Either you worked in the tobacco fields, became a butler or worked with the horses on the horse farm. None of those jobs paid us all that much and I admired your grandfather, so I learned to work with the horses.

In those days you had to work as a farm hand cleaning stalls and bailing hay. Those were the only horse farm jobs we were allowed to have. Back then, your grandfather was a stable hand for Mr. J.W. Young and his farm in North Middletown. I used to help him like you are helping me now.

Over time, your grandfather became very close with a horse named Brown Sugar. They had themselves this real special bond. I remember as a young kid, right about your age in fact, listening to your grandfather talk to Brown Sugar as if he were his own son."

"Apple doesn't fall far from the tree does it Dad?" I interrupt softly with a childish grin.

Taking his eyes off the competition he turns to me, "I guess not. But I can't hold a candle to your grandfather and his love for the horses... especially Brown Sugar.

Although you never knew your grandfather, he was the one that taught me the importance of a bond with the horses. He always said the horses will give you a peace of mind no human can ever give you. He also told me that many of life's lessons can be learned working with the horses. These are the same things I'm trying to pass on to you. Like I'm always telling you, the most difficult things in life are always the right things in life."

I could tell by Dad's tone he is serious and not in a sharp kind of way, but enough that the importance of his points cannot be understated. I continue listening intently, as he continues to speak, "I learned that from your grandfather. Even though he was a poor farm hand, he was rich in wisdom to tell me to watch and learn the riding skills of the owners. Your grandfather told me that if I really wanted to be a horseman... beyond a farm hand, I needed to learn by watching."

Listening to Dad made me lose focus to all else around me. Instances with this type of openness were rare, yet here we are, in the moment. They say imitation is the finest form of flattery and in that story I learned that his Dad used horses to teach him the same life lessons he is now teaching me. To try and lighten the emotion I ask, "So how come you and Momma don't want me working horses?"

"To be honest son," Dad replies, "The world is a big place and has a lot to offer. We just want you to do your best. I love horses. Did from the day I was born it seems. Your grandfather wanted me to do better than him in my life, just like me and your Momma want for you. He wanted me to become an independent man on my own and defy white peoples' thinking that our people could not be successful. He wanted me to overcome the obstacles of being a deprived Negro like the great boxer Jack Johnson did."

"And like Jackie Robinson did?" I ask.

"Exactly. Like Jackie Robinson too. But I love these horses too much and on the day your grandfather died, I prayed to both him and God above to help me learn to ride and train these horses. I prayed to God that if I would someday ride and train these horses I could do something good."

Dad then mentioned how around the time Grandfather died, Mr. Young also died leaving his son Stoddard Young to run the farm. He then added how he worked as a horse trainer apprentice under Stoddard Young for over twenty years. During those days, he worked with some of the best known Saddlebred horses in the country including Admiration of the Nation, Minute Man, Spray of the Sea and Richlieu's Fashion.

"Years later," Dad continues, "My prayers were answered when Dr. Bachtel gave me a chance to train his horses. I explained to Dr. Bachtel when he hired me that I could help him win the shows if he allowed me to train his horses. He agreed and that's what I have done ever since.

As nice as Doc is to me it's only 'cause I train these horses real good for him. The bottom line is Bulgia is right too, our people will never amount to anything in this white man's world. Years later when people look back, they'll remember the great horses... and maybe even who owns them. But they'll never know the men who trained them. No, we will all be forgotten."

Those words hit me roughly, as if someone tossed a brick against my head. I hoped Dad would be wrong... hoped that someday someone would remember all he and the other horsemen had done. All the people in these stands are witnessing the beauty and grace by these large animals, and it is truly amazing. Could they all forget?

As I ponder these thoughts, I see the first class of the fine harness horses exiting the ring. In our conversation, the entire event passed and in a rush, Dad runs over to Dr. Bachtel to help him out of the carriage.

"What happened?" I ask Uncle JT as we approach the horses.

"We didn't do too well in this one. Ambassador showed well, but not good enough, but we still have Next To My Heart in the next class," he replies.

"Wow... I thought for sure Ambassador would place well. He looked so good in practice yesterday."

"Well, as we've all been saying, the competition is real tough. Besides, The Lemon Drop Kid was competing."

"Who's that?"

Pointing over to one of the large horses strapped in to a carriage, Uncle JT replies, "That one right there. Already won three national championships, and gearing for its fourth later this year. Heck, once I saw him in the field I knew it was all over. That's one rare horse."

Looking the horse over, I do seem to notice a difference. He is a 'man' among 'boys', a superstar among stars. I found out later that The Lemon Drop Kid did end up winning four consecutive Fine Harness Grand Championships and ended up becoming one of the most popular horses of the time.

A short time later in the second class it was Next To My Heart's chance at the Fine Harness. As I watched her go through the event, she looked much stronger than she did the day before in practice. Unfortunately, the competition was top notch and she also did not place to the championship round. So with two preliminary events over, we were batting .500 and the final event, the five gait later this evening will make or break this competition for The Dells Farm. I know we are all happy with Painted Doll moving on to the next day, but if we could qualify in two of the three events, we will all be extremely excited for our good fortune.

Chapter 15

Early that evening as dusk arrives, it is time to start preparing King Cloud for the final event of the day, the five gait. Though the fine harness is important and the three gait is exciting, the fanfare surrounding the five gait echoes far beyond just our stable house.

In this event, the colors of the stable are intertwined within the horse's mane and tail, and the colors look especially vibrant under the large lights that overcast the competition ring. In addition, with the overall popularity of the event, success in the five gait can carry a farm for a long while. It is the cream of the entire Canfield's American Saddlebred show and as such, even this evening's qualifying rounds are met with heightened anticipation.

King Cloud is competing in the first class and Dr. Bachtel is going to ride him. Mrs. Bachtel and Hot Toddy are in the fourth and final class, giving us about an hour between the two. In preparation of the class qualifiers, I am holding the burgundy and gold ribbon in hand as Dad is carefully braiding King Cloud's mane and tail. As with the stable tack, the colorful uniformity of the colors bring reference to our Dells Farm on show day.

While Dad is weaving the thick, vibrant ribbon in with the horse hair, Uncle JT brushes King Cloud's mane and tail while all along we sing together in tune with the hi-fi.

" Do you know why we add the ribbons in?" Dad asks when there is a break in the music.

"To make the horses look pretty I'd guess..." I reply with hesitation as Dad interweaves the horse's hair and the ribbon, two strands of the former to one of the latter, maneuvered together with a lightening fast perfection. His hands move rhythmically like that of a seasoned magician. He braids King Cloud's mane in small, separate pieces and the caramel brown color of the horse's mane with the burgundy and gold ribbon are a perfect match.

"That they sure do. What you think Country Boy?"

"I'd agree with the boy there Mojo. Sure does make the horse look even prettier..."

Dad then continues with his task, now lacing King Cloud's tail but with only one braid. Momma always said Dad could braid hair better than any woman could and he could do it with his eyes closed. Watching him braid King Cloud first hand, I could see she was right. Dad seldom even looked while braiding the hair and spoke of the natural feeling and maneuvering of the fingers and hands being similar to maneuvering the reins while riding a horse. I always enjoyed watching Dad braid because it was so perfectly done and in the end, the ribbon would be evenly distributed with the horse's hair.

After finishing, Dad and Uncle JT throw over King Cloud a burgundy and gold woven blanket with the Bachtel farm logo on the rear. Dad then wraps King's legs with the white cotton leg padding and covers that with the burgundy and gold color padding bands.

Dr. Bachtel arrives in the same suit he had on earlier, accented with riding boots and silver spurs, and a wide burgundy and gold ban around the base of his fedora. He also has a white carnation in his suit lapel. Beside him is Mrs. Bachtel, looking as primed as ever.

Dad then gives Dr. Bachtel a tan, two-foot baton stiff whip. As he does he says, "Now Doc, there ain't no need to use this at all. Just wave it close to King's right ear and he will know it's there and respond."

"Sounds good Tom," Dr. Bachtel replies.

Without any further conversation, we all exit the barn together. Dad leads King Cloud while Uncle JT and I follow him. The four of us are led together by the Bachtel's who are leading our progression. While we make our way to the show ring, most of the other horses have already arrived. Just like King Cloud, all the other horses are also decked out in the colors of their stables.

Just then, everyone is notified to mount-up onto their horses. In addition to the Bachtel's, I see Pete Jones dressed in a brown suit, a shade darker than his light brown skin tone, resting upon a beautiful gray horse.

"What's that horse's name?" I ask my Dad as I point to the horse Pretty Boy is riding, but I do not get an answer in response.

I turn around and see Dad has made his way off to the side and is standing beside Sweet Mary, the horse from yesterday. He is patting her side tenderly while looking down at her lower legs. It is then when the same man from yesterday meets up with Dad. I am too far away to hear their words, but I can see Dad is visibly upset. After a short conversation, he quickly walks away from the man and back over to where we are standing.

" What happened?" Uncle JT asks as the horses begin to follow the ringmaster's instructions.

"The ignorant bastard is soring her. No wonder she was freaking out yesterday."

"Man," Uncle JT responds shaking his head in sorrow, "that's just wrong."

At the moment, I am a bit lost. I could not recall ever seeing Dad this angry before and I have no idea what soring means. Half afraid to speak, but wanting to know more I ask in a whisper, "Um… what exactly is soring? Is it bad?"

"Real bad," Uncle JT responds.

"Son," Dad then adds, "Sweet Mary was one fine horse when she was with us and he is breaking her." He pauses for a moment before continuing to answer my question, "Anyway, soring is a cruel trick used to force a horse's gait. A bad trainer like that bastard over there will irritate or blister a horse's forelegs, usually by rubbing on a hot chemical… bleach, acid, or somethin' like it."

I cannot envision such cruelty. As I am dealing with the information, Uncle JT adds, "And most times sored horses develop permanent scars because of it."

I still cannot believe it, which causes me to ask, "Why? What good can come from that?"

"When the horse walks after she's been sored, it responds quickly by lifting its front legs to relieve the pain. That quick motion looks great when doing the gait. So, many horse owners and trainers who want to improve their horse's chances of winning at shows use soring as an unfair shortcut. Its sick, that's what it is," Dad replies.

After finishing, Dad just shakes his head in disgust and exhales a long sigh in attempt to calm himself down.

"Let's just watch the show," Uncle JT says soothingly.

As the three of us go to the side of the grandstand around the ring to watch the competition, the first class of horses make their way into the ring. In this class, both King Cloud and Sweet Mary are showing.

We all turn our attention to the ring, but I can tell the sight of Sweet Mary in progression with the other horses is a constant reminder to my Dad's anger.

For the next fifteen minutes or so, we all watch in silence as the first class of qualifying horses run through their performance, following the commands of the ringmaster over the microphone. The lights of the event are in full power, accenting the magical movements of the horses and their riders.

As I am watching, King Cloud stands out in my eye and looks amazing. Like in the three gait, Dad rushes on to the grassy infield to help Dr. Bachtel with the saddle. Looking on, I can see why this event is the premier one. The horses all seem more regal as they perform their routines and it is as if they are walking on air. King Cloud definitely lives up to his name in this event.

As the judges are inspecting each horse, I see one stop and look down at Sweet Mary, which causes me to ask, "Do they take off points or anything for the soring?"

"Unfortunately not," Uncle JT responds. "It is completely legal. To make matters worse, it's gaining popularity. Sad ain't it."

"Yeah," I say as I look upon Sweet Mary with a bit of remorse. I would find out years later that in 1970 the Horse Protection Act was instilled to help prevent the future practice of soring as a means to accentuate a horse's gait.

My thoughts move back to the event as the ringmaster speaks once again, "Alright Ladies and Gentlemen, let's here it for all our competitors."

The crowd, which is now at full capacity all clap in accordance. The ringmaster then continues, "Unfortunately, only the top three in this class can move on to tomorrow's championship round. After a brief pause he announces, "Our first finalist is Lucky Guy, ridden by C.C. Turner of Founders

Farms in North Plainfield, New Jersey."

The crowd erupts into a controlled applause as the light tan horse moves forward to claim his qualifying ribbon. We look on with an understated tenseness coursing through our veins. With our collective breath held, we listen patiently for the ringmaster to signify the next qualifier.

"Our next finalist is King Cloud, ridden by Dr. David Bachtel of The Dells Farm from North Canton, Ohio."

The clapping from the crowd continues as Dr. Bachtel trots King Cloud forward to receive his qualifying ribbon. The exhilaration within Dad, Uncle JT and I is without restraint. Befitting of my youthful exuberance, I cheer and jump in excitement. At first, the reaction embarrasses me, but when I see Uncle JT and Dad react similarly, my uncomfortable anxiety vanishes.

The ringmaster then once more speaks into his microphone "And finally, Sweet Mary, ridden by John Kelly from Kelly Farms in Covington, Kentucky. Will you please step forward?"

Upon hearing her name, both Uncle JT and I turn to Dad to see how he reacts. It is obvious he is torn in two directions. Happy the horse is finding success, but angry at the price she has to pay. It seems though the time has been good for him and he is now much calmer than he was before.

The crowd cheers as the first qualifying class is over. In a rush, we run over and greet Dr. Bachtel, who is already celebrating with Mrs. Bachtel. After a quick congratulations from all around, Dad turns to Uncle JT and says, "Alright, lets bring King back and get Hot Toddy ready."

"Sounds good," Uncle JT replies with a wave of enthusiasm born of the day's success.

"Let's get Hot Toddy lookin' real good. I want Mrs. B to have a good showing..."

"How come?" I ask as we begin to take King Cloud back to the stable. "I mean, we already got one horse into tomorrow's final round. What's it matter?"

Dad stops for a moment, turns and says, "It's a matter of pride. Don't matter that we got one horse in... might as well shoot for two. Beside you are always gonna want to try to do your best. Mrs. B ain't going out there to fail and Hot Toddy has worked real hard for this moment too. We all wanna win..."

Listening to Dad's words, I understand what he is saying. We bring King Cloud back, cool him down and just short of an hour later the Bachtel's return to our tack and we move to the ring with Hot Toddy. As he did with Dr. Bachtel, Dad gives Mrs. Bachtel a leg up on the horse and soon thereafter we take our familiar position to watch as the event starts.

While Hot Toddy and Mrs. Bachtel are representing the Dells, I can see their passion. It is obvious that both horse and rider go through their routine with a concentrated sense of crispness and perfection. As this is happening, I hear Uncle JT getting some of the results from the earlier classes. Most of the names I don't recognize, but a select few I do. Uncle Bill's horse Kentucky Sunrise, Pretty Boy's Earl Gray, and Bulgia's horse Shades of Blue all made it to the championship round tomorrow. In all, the event was fantastic for the Mighty Middletown Horsemen.

It takes a little over twenty minutes for the twelve horses in this class to go through their routine. Mrs. Bachtel is a skilled rider and her talent shines through even though she is on a horse other than Painted Doll. Unfortunately, for all her efforts and despite the clean routine by Hot Toddy, the pair does not finish in the top three.

After the event ends and as the stands begin to clear out, Uncle JT and I catch up with Dad who is already talking with Dr. Bachtel.

"Great work today Tom on all the horses. Especially on King Cloud. The whip worked just as you said. I didn't have to use it once."

"You got yourself a real special horse there," Dad replies with a warm and thankful smile.

Turning to Mrs. Bachtel, Dad says, "You and Hot Toddy looked real good out there too."

"We sure did. David is just lucky we didn't move on to the final round. I was looking forward to whipping him," she replies coyly.

"That I am," Dr. Bachtel counters with a wry laughter. "I don't think we would have beat you." After a brief pause, "Well good work gentlemen," Dr. Bachtel then says to us as he holds his wife tightly. "Eileen and I are going to go talk with the other owners. Two final rounds... very exciting."

"Sounds good. We will get these horses all cooled and bedded down. Painted Doll and King Cloud will be ready to go for you tomorrow."

With that, Dr. Bachtel grabs Dad's hand in a firm grasp and gives it a good shake while saying, "Again... good job today Tom."

Dad thanks him and as the Bachtel's leave, Dad grabs the reins to Hot Toddy and we head back for the day's final chores.

Chapter 16

Sunday

We awoke Sunday morning with anticipation encompassing our silent thoughts. The night before, the horsemen stayed up later than they did Thursday or Friday evening, waxing and waning in conversation about the day's events, and what today's championship rounds will bring. In all, nine of the black horsemen, with Dad included among them, had horses move on to theses final rounds in at least one of the three events. It seems of all, Pretty Boy had the most success as in each event, he and the farm he trained for were well represented in the championship round. Beyond him, Tom Butler's and Stanley Jackson's farms placed in two events. The remaining five, the Stivers Brothers, Uncle Bill, Bulgia, Ted Morris, and Beauford Hall each qualified in one final round event. In all, the Mighty Middletown Horseman had a very productive Saturday and even in its success, it would not be considered a landmark. Success was expected and this was surely not the first time many of them had done well.

Upon awaking this cool, dark morning, Uncle JT, Dad and I begin our morning routine in near silence, reflecting in private our thoughts about the coming day. Last night was about the horsemen, but today it is about the Dells Farm.

To some extent, our weekend could be viewed as successful. With Painted Doll in the three gait and King Cloud in the five, two of our best and most successful horses will have an opportunity to win their championship events. If we can get a top five finish in either, Dr. Bachtel will likely consider the entire weekend a success. If we could do so in both events, it would be a major coup. Though we all want to win, as any competitor may, to a man each of the Mighty Middletown Horsemen are looking for the favor of light to shine upon them or another. Success for all is just as desired in these circles. Although it may not be of the owners' aspiration, the horsemen still all want to see the others do well. It is within that conception where our thoughts rest this morning.

The morning events followed as closely to the others here and all went without incident. Breakfast had with it a somber undertone. The nuances of human emotion are lost on me at the age of ten but as I aged and other 'big' events came before me, I understood the mood we all were feeling this day. Excitement, apprehension and even a twinge of euphoria were all mixed within us, but each emotion took a back seat to the presence of the day itself.

For the most part, all our jobs are done. Sure Dad has a bit more work during the competitions and we still needed to prepare the horses before the events and cool them afterwards, but essentially the fate of the day's progression lies mostly in the hands of the two horses we are resting our hopes upon.

As the morning light tries to lay full bloom over the fairgrounds, its ambient rays are held back by the soft gray clouds of storm held over from last night. The forecast calls for clear skies throughout the day, but as I look upward I think nature has a ways to go to meet such a lofty goal.

By about eight, we have completed our morning routine. With an hour to go to the first event of the day, Uncle JT, Dad and I are just completing Painted Doll's morning pampering. With Sam Cooke lending a sense of familiarity echoing out from the hi-fi, the tension has since been lifted and our conversation, though light and without meaning has a weighted significance in the fact it keeps the normality of the morning steadfast. The importance of the music for both the trainers and the horses cannot be trivialized.

I once asked Dad why he always played music in the stables… and especially Sam Cooke so often. He told me that the music not only kept the horses calm, but the trainers too. Within all the horse stables, there is a lot of pressure to keep the horses in good shape and performing well… especially on big weekends such as this one. The music enabled the horsemen's uneasy minds to stay relaxed and focused. As for Sam Cooke, he was just Dad's favorite.

He also told me numerous times how horses can sense the apprehension within a man and that is one of the reasons a rider's tension can make or break an event. Given that, it is imperative for the trainers to remain as calm and at ease as possible, and the music helped make that happen.

With the event only minutes away, we begin to move Painted Doll to the main ring where each of the final three events will take place. Walking toward the ring, I find myself appreciating the morning. The smell of the morning concessions has become second nature, but I still find myself yearning for Momma's home cooking.

The scent of freshly cut grass overpowers the scent of food the nearer we get to the ring. Mentioning this to Dad, he relays to me that in fact, the grass probably has not been trimmed for two or three days. However, because of the morning's light precipitation, the fragrance spawns a fresh cut scent. He further goes on to say that even though the infield grass may be damp, last night's and this morning's drizzle would unlikely distract the horses in the show.

Approaching the front entrance to the ring, we see many of the owners milling about, engaged in conversation and examining each horse with a careful eye. When we arrive, about two thirds of the event's contestants are already here, including Dr. and Mrs. Bachtel.

" Hello Tom," Dr. Bachtel says to Dad with an outstretched hand. "We looking good this morning?"

"Yes sir," Dad replies as he warmly greets his boss. "Painted Doll is primed and ready to go. I think she's real excited."

"Of course she is," Mrs. Bachtel adds as she approaches the horse. "She knows exactly what's going on today... Don't you girl?" she finishes as she nuzzles her nose against the horse.

It is obvious she loves the horse and to me it is refreshing to see. Dad always made it a point to explain how many of the owners care only about winning and very little about the horses themselves. In the case of Mrs. Bachtel however, whose love for the horses is obvious, she has been the rare and refreshing exception. It is no wonder they make such a good team.

In today's final, championship round, the twelve best horses, or at least best in the judges' eyes, will compete. The top five horses will place and the remaining seven will leave with nothing but mention in the final results and the qualifying ribbon they received yesterday. It is our goal, as it is the goal of each of the twelve finalists, to obviously end up in the top five. With that being said, the air is thick with the tension of competition.

"How are you doing honey? Are you ready?" Dr. Bachtel asks his wife as he massages her shoulders gently.

"I am. I have a good feeling..." she replies with a confident smile.

"Just stay patient with her," Dad interjects. "Painted Doll will take care of you."

"She always does," Mrs. Bachtel replies while issuing a final pat on the horse's side.

After wishing Mrs. Bachtel good luck, Dad interlocks his fingers and gives her a makeshift step, helping her onto the horse. Painted Doll shakes her head in excitement, fully aware of who just mounted her. After Mrs. Bachtel is comfortably atop the steed, the rest of us take our positions beyond the outer railing as we did yesterday.

While the contestants are all lining up, I question Dad about the judges and what traits they are looking for when examining the horses. Having watched yesterday's events and having seen the horses practice numerous times before, I knew the obvious criteria the judges used for the performance of the various gaits. However, what I longed to know and what Dad answered were instead the other intangibles they look for. I am surprised to hear the depth of his answer.

"Well son," Dad starts in as we watch the horses. "There are four things these judges will be lookin' for in the horses: balance, structure, muscle and quality. They use these four areas so there can be a common system at all the shows. It sure does make it easier on us trainers too, since we know exactly what to focus on.

Now, balance is probably the most important piece of the bunch, but is also the most difficult to understand. Most people usually think balance has to do with a horse's ability to keep posture, but that's really not what the judges are looking for. Instead, balance is the way a horse's parts fit together to form the whole. It's usually judged from the side view, about thirty feet away from the horse."

"What do they look at to judge this?" I ask.

"Pretty much the topline, back, hip and neck of the horse," Dad replies.

He then goes on to continue telling me that starting with the overall balance of the horse, one should be able to draw three equal circles on the horse's body. One circle should start at the point of the shoulder and extending to the heartgirth. A second circle should be made behind the heartgirth to the flank and the final one at the flank to the point of the buttocks.

As I try to make sense of it, Dad simply tells me to close my eyes and just visualize the circles in my head, as that would help provide a starting point in evaluating balance.

"Can you see it in your head? Imagine the circles on Painted Doll."

I nod as the sight becomes clear in my mind's eye.

"Good, now. As you are looking at the circles I want you to ask yourself, are all the circles the same size? Which circle is smallest? Which circle is largest?"

I open my eyes, and compare the imaginary circles with those on the real Painted Doll, who is now in routine with the other eleven contestants following the instructions of the announcer. Her circles are very even and upon noticing that, I see how balanced she really is.

Ecstatic at the insight, I listen as Dad continues. He proceeds, although with not as much detail as he did with the balance, the basic characteristics of the other three major areas judges look at.

"As for the horse's structure, it's pretty much judged from three positions: the side, front and rear views. But, for a horse to perform right it must have sound feet and legs.

You see, blemishes don't count because that just comes with the horses. They may detract from the horse's appearance, but doesn't really hurt his ability to show," Dad continues.

"What counts as a blemish then?" I wonder aloud.

"A lot of things really. Wire cuts, rope burns, shoe boils, and so on. It is because of this that soring technically doesn't lower a horse's score."

I see that even mentioning the subject really pains my dad. Then continuing on as the horses are performing their trots around the outer ring, Dad points out the importance of the muscles within the horses and how the judges score them.

Years later when researching more information about the judging procedures, I learned even more details than what Dad shared with me that morning. For example, since all movement originates from the contraction and relaxation of muscle, the horse depends on muscle for a variety of functions. Locomotion, running the heart, and even to move certain parts of its body to chase away flies are some of the major duties of a horse's muscles. The judges look to see that certain areas of the body possess additional volume and definition of muscling. In evaluating muscle, both quality and quantity are important in all breeds. The most desirable kind of muscling is long, smooth and deep tying rather than short and bunchy.

After Dad finishes explaining about the horses muscle and what the judges look for when considering it, our attention focuses back to the competition itself. Looking out at the contestants, Painted Doll is performing with a perfect style and grace... or at least it seems so to my untrained eyes. By the time the horses fall into their line-up on the infield grass, the crowd is glued to them. Silence permeates, except for a few soft whispers of animated conversations surely touting private opinions on which horse is best.

"This is where they are reviewing the horse's quality," Dad says as the judges take their time examining the horses.

"Like how good they pose?" I ask, thinking the obvious.

"Kind of. Quality is looked at like a mixture of the skin, hair, head, feet and so on. If the horse is to be of a high quality, kinda like Painted Doll is, it'll have smooth, short hair and thin skin. On the head, the ears will be short and stand at attention."

I also later learned in my studies that there were some additional things which can make a horse be thought of as high quality. Those being the face is short and displays width between the eyes, tapering to a fine muzzle. The eyes being prominent and located on the corners of the face to permit a greater range of vision. The joints being free of swelling or puffiness and the skin fitting smoothly over the joints. And finally, the feet being medium sized and well rounded at the front, with width and depth at the heel.

As Dad finishes, the horses all begin to take their steps backwards, one by one on the judges' command prior to the dismounting segment of the competition. Listening to his words, I looked at a few of the horses to judge these characteristics as best as possible with my own eye. To me, all the horses seem to have high quality and it makes me admire the judges' ability to differentiate between them all.

With his explanation of the judging done, Dad makes his way to the center of the ring to help Mrs. Bachtel with the saddle when it is Painted Doll's turn for the conformation.

With the judging going on, the Mighty Middletown Horsemen are represented well. Of the twelve finalists, four of the horses are from within Dad's group of friends. One third of the finalists of nearly fifty entrants is a strong showing. It is not just the aura of these men that lays tale to their history being written by the actions they live, but the success they find in doing so.

After each horse has had the opportunity to impress the judges in both form and motion, the ringmaster dictates into his microphone, "Ladies and Gentlemen, what a performance this morning. Wouldn't you all agree?"

The crowd reveals a wave of applause, showing their approval for the fine performances by all the horses. Uncle JT tenses with excitement, as does Dr. Bachtel who is standing on the other side of me. Their hands are both clench the railing with a renewed vigor. Waiting for judges to come to their conclusions, the fairgrounds now finds itself in a hush, as if the grandstand itself is holding it breath.

After the judges walk over and hand the results to the ringmaster, he steps forward to the microphone to address the crowd.

"Ladies and Gentlemen, let's give a hand to each of these fine horses and their riders."

On his words, the crowd erupts in a rhythmic clapping. Then, continuing on the ringmaster says, "Our fifth place winner of $200 is Smooth Velvet, ridden by David Hobbs of Charmer Farmer located in Harrisburg, Pennsylvania."

Smooth Velvet is a maple colored horse, with a flowing mane longer than most of the other horses in the competition. The horse is also of a fairy large stature and by the details Dad had told me, is of high quality.

After the horse nears the front of the grandstand and receives its trophy, pink ribbon and check, the ringmaster continues.

"In forth place and receiving a $250 prize is Holiday Dream, ridden by Pete Jones of Miller and Miller Farms."

As the crowd begins its cheers, I look over at Uncle JT and see he is very happy. Success for any of the horsemen is welcomed and in support of his friend, he cheers with enthusiasm.

After Pretty Boy receives his trophy, white ribbon and check, the ringmaster continues, "The third place winner of

$300.00 is Voodoo Daddy, ridden by Bruce Carnes of Pleasant Meadow farms located in Lynchburg, Virginia."

Standing behind the horse Voodoo Daddy, I recognize one of the trainers, but cannot place his name. Leaning in I ask Uncle JT, "Who's that trainer?"

"That's Slick Wess," he replies. "He's one of us too. We are sure lookin' good."

Mr. Carnes slowly trots Voodoo Daddy to the front of the grandstand and halts the horse where a judge presents him with the yellow third place ribbon and small trophy and check. The grandstand audience applauses politely as Mr. Carnes tips his hat and accepts his prize and rides half way around the ring to the exit as the other two winners did before him.

"The second place winner," the announcer starts up again after Voodoo Daddy has exited the ring, "And earner of the $400 prize is Southern Belle, ridden by Ashley Turnbull of Hickory Creek Farms from Lexington, Kentucky."

This was the horse that showed so much promise yesterday, and is of no surprise to anyone. The stands show their appreciation for the horse with a whole-hearty response as Mr. Turnbull rides forward to accept the prize and the second place red ribbon.

Eight horses remain and among them still is Painted Doll. The tension is high for all the remaining farms, because only one will come away with the top blue ribbon prize and for the rest, nothing at all.

As the ringmaster begins to speak one last time to announce the first place winner, the sounds of the fairgrounds come to a complete halt. The remaining horses are standing in the halt-firm form in the infield as we all listen to the ringmaster's voice radiating from the microphone, "And the winner of the $500 victory prize is Painted Doll, ridden by Mrs. Eileen Bachtel for The Dells Farm of North Canton, Ohio!"

Looking at Dad, I can see a smile as wide and long as the Mississippi River resting on his face. He is beaming a proud radiance as any father would for their child, though even in my youth I can tell his emotion is not for me. Moreover it does not matter, for as Painted Doll is like a daughter to him, she has very much become like a half-sister to me. We share the same father and as the crowd applauds her, I find a sense of accomplishment filling me and I know it is shared with everyone in the Dells camp.

"Great work out there," Dad says to Mrs. Bachtel as Uncle JT and I meet up with the group.

"It was more her than me," she replies as she pats Painted doll. "But we thank you anyway."

On those words, Dr. Bachtel helps his wife off the horse and embraces her. It is a fantastic moment to share without a doubt. We all hoped, but I do not think any of us imagined a first place victory. It is a powerful experience.

On the way back to the barn after the event, we walk Painted Doll back the long way. The long cool down walk is an old good luck superstition. This cool down procedure had been the same for every horse so far and with two progressions to the championship round and one first place victory already, there is no need to change what has been working.

Dad explains to me the importance of cooling down is beyond good luck, as you need to work on getting the horse's temperature, pulse rate and respiration rate back to normal. After arriving back to the stable's exterior, our first task is to remove her saddle. I am about to remove the saddle cloth as Uncle JT is hanging the heavy leather saddle away, when Dad places his hand on mine and urges me to stop.

He tells me that it is best to keep the saddlecloth on for a bit longer, to help cool the horse down. In the meantime, I should serve Painted Doll some water. In her zest to drink, she laps it up without hesitation as her tongue splashes some of the cool water on all of us around her.

After Painted Doll is cool and her thirst has been quenched, we remove the saddlecloth and being a hot day, hose her down with cool water. As we have done the entire weekend, we bathe her down and upon finishing, towel dry her affectionately. Because of her recent victory, we give her a little extra pampering, all the while congratulating her on her good showing.

She takes to it openly and seems to understand our praise. Clearly, she earns every bit of it. From the talk among the horsemen last night, the opposition at these events has been among the most competitive in a long while. To even place is a major accomplishment and Painted Doll was able to manage even more than that. It was a victory that was simply exhilarating.

Just as we finish with Painted Doll, Dr. and Mrs. Bachtel arrive at the stable, and with them they bring a bountiful excitement.

"Gentlemen," Dr. Bachtel says as he edges up to the tack. "I think we need to flaunt these…"

"Now honey," Mrs. Bachtel interrupts with a smile.

Before she can say anything else, Dr. Bachtel continues, "Lee, why don't you turn up the hi-fi."

I follow his instructions as he then continues, "Tom, why don't you help me hang this first place blue ribbon."

"Yes sir," Dad replies with a smile. He walks over and holds up the ribbon while Dr. Bachtel attaches it with the other ribbons… though in a centered and prominent position.

They do the same with the trophy and over the next few minutes, we revel in the festivity of our success. Time seems to stop, as does the world around us. In that moment, Dad, Uncle JT, Dr and Mrs. Bachtel, the horses and I all celebrate together.

Chapter 17

A few hours after the three-gait event, we have long since finished the initial celebrations of Painted Doll's victory. The stable house had a cloud of cheerfulness hanging within it, invigorating all of us.

In hindsight, the fact Painted Doll did so well should not have been a surprise to any of us. As Silver Rocket, she was a champion and then even more so after her transformation into Painted Doll. In reality, the horse is and always has been a winner. Considering Mrs. Bachtel rode her was an important factor. Not to say anything against Dr. Bachtel, but his wife has a certain connection with the horse, often leading the Dells' Farm to victory. Moreover, in the championship round today it surely showed.

After our early afternoon chores, I wondered what we would be doing next. Unfortunately, not having placed in the fine harness event, Dad, Uncle JT and I did not go to the championship round. This surprised me as I thought we would at least go to support the other horsemen. In addition, I was curious to see which horses would win. When asking him why we were not going his reply was two-fold.

Since we were not competing in the Fine Harness, we could us the extra time to prepare for the five gait. With the event not until the evening time, we will have plenty of opportunity to make sure King Cloud and all his tack equipment looks its best. The reins need to be oiled and polished, as does the halter and saddle.

"Also," he adds with a whisper. "I have a surprise for you..."

Just then, I hear a familiar voice say out from the doorway, "How ya doin' baby. You mindin' your Daddy?"

Upon hearing the voice, I turn in excitement and see my momma and my Aunts Kat and Julie entering the stable. Dressed in a long yellow sundress with a blue floral print, Momma is a welcome sight. Until seeing her, I could not believe how much I had actually missed her this weekend. In a hurry, I immediately run over and give her a big hug.

Then, turning beside her, I give both Aunt Kat and Aunt Julie a warm embrace as well, equally excited to see the both of them.

" Hello darlin'," Aunt Julie says to me, also clothed in a warm-colored sundress.

Looking up I ask them all, "So what are you doing here? I sure didn't expect it!"

"Well," Dad says answering my question, "They are coming by tonight for the little party us trainers throw after every show. And since we had a little extra time today I thought they could come by early, have lunch and watch King in the five."

"That's right honey," Momma says. "So how you been doin' out here? Workin' hard?"

"I am. And we did real well in the three gait today. Painted Doll won first place."

"Really? That's real good. You must bring some good luck to the Dells here."

"He sure did," Uncle JT interjects as he enters the stable. "Hello Kat," he then adds with a large smile. The moment is awkward, warm and friendly all at once. Uncle JT is very shy around Aunt Kat because of his desires for her affection.

"So Kat," Dad asks already knowing the answer, "You are staying for the party tonight, right?"

Looking at Uncle JT, Aunt Kat replies, "I sure am. Wouldn't miss it for anything."

"Sounds good. Hopefully we can get Country Boy here to dance right and not do that skank dance he always does."

"C'mon now Mojo" Uncle JT retorts, "You know you practice it when I'm not around." On those words, he then breaks out into the full-body shake, mimicking his own dance.

The rest of us laugh out, unable to control the jubilant energy. Uncle JT has always been a joker and with the success of the morning, he just feeds off of the liveliness of the day. The six of us get lunch soon thereafter and we fill the ladies in on the weekend's events thus far. With a fiery zest, I explain to them how much I learned about the horses and the horsemen, training and cooling techniques, and even about the competitions themselves.

The lunch is the best I've had here so far. Having nothing to do with the food itself, but instead being able to share it with Momma and my Aunts is an amazing feeling.

After eating, Momma and my two Aunts tour the fairgrounds as Dad, Uncle JT and I have more work to do to get ready for the evening's big event. Though the three gait was amazing and our victory should not at all be minimized, the five gait championship round is the World Series, game seven of the events this weekend... and we all want King Cloud to do well. The competition will be even more difficult than that in the three and we want the equipment and the horse to be at their best.

One of my chores is to give King Cloud's saddle a good rubdown. Using a bar of saddle soap, I have to clean out the pores of the leather from all the dirt and excess oil. It is imperative the leather remains clean. It takes a lot of hard work, but in the end the preservation of the leather makes the effort worthwhile.

"Do you remember how to do this?" Dad asks as he hands me the bar of soap and a sponge.

"Of course," I respond. "I'm gonna soap up the saddle, then wipe it clean with a sponge. As long as the soap suds keep turning gray, I need to keep cleaning."

"Very good. I'll also need you to condition that saddle. Can you do that too?"

"Um sure," I say sheepishly, "But I'm not exactly sure what that is all about."

Dad pats me on the back as a large grin forms on his face. He then says, "Conditioning is only necessary if your leather is thirsty, which this saddle most definitely is. But you certainly don't want to over-condition it to the point that it feels too oily. Pretty much just rub in some of this here oil to replenish the leather. You want to do it before it completely dries though. If it dries out completely after you soap it, the leather will feel like an old board. When it's almost dry, put the oil on it."

For the next thirty minutes we work, cleaning and polishing all King Cloud's saddle along with halter and bridle one last time. Not only will King Cloud look his best, but so will all the equipment that will adorn him.

Chapter 18

Early evening arrives and with it comes baited breath. The fairgrounds are now filled to capacity, resembling a summer state fair. The darkened sky is illuminated for miles around by the large halogen lights, rising high into the star-filled atmosphere. A cool breeze blows through the entirety of the fairgrounds, channeled by the large barns and whistling against the metal of the grandstand's bleachers.

The show is to start at eight o'clock and is the final event of the weekend. As we are cleaning and preparing King Cloud's saddle and other tack equipment, Dad speaks faintly as he talks about the importance of this event. He reminds me that no matter how it turns out, the weekend should be considered a success for reasons beyond that of even Painted Doll's victory. No one could argue his assessment of this weekend.

However, the prestige of the five gait is more so than any of the other events. Therefore, coming in the top five would set this weekend apart from most others. Dr. Bachtel did not put any stipulations on the event, as he was ecstatic about the success the Dells accomplished so far. Nevertheless, even I knew winning in the championship round of the five gait would speak volumes about the Dells Farm and Dad's ability as a horseman.

Uncle JT brings King Cloud out from his stall to begin his pre-event grooming process and over the next few minutes, Dad once again braids King Cloud's mane and tail.

"You know Country Boy, it amazes me," Dad says aloud as he braids the mane of King Cloud. The deftness of his technique still keeps me in awe. His fingers are leathered and hardened from the years of working the horses, yet he is able to manipulate the vibrant cloth with a surgeon's skill.

"What's that Mojo," Uncle JT replies.

"It amazes me how calm King Cloud stays. I got the butterflies in my stomach and I'm not the one whose gonna be in front of all those people."

"Maybe he doesn't realize what's gonna happen," I interject.

Before I can say another word, both men look at me and say together in stereo, "Oh... he knows..."

"You're right Mojo, it sure is amazin'," Uncle JT then finishes.

As I continue to brush the horse, we all further engage in simplistic conversation as to not break Dad's concentration too much. Uncle JT then moves across the room and gets the hi-fi playing. The calming tunes of Fats Domino echo its soul-filling reverberation and like King Cloud, I find my nerves eased by it all.

While the preparation is going on, Dr. Bachtel walks into the stable, entering with a confident swagger. This evening, he is wearing a finely pressed, light gray suit, accented by a beautiful white orchid pinned to the lapel. Resting on his head is a matching off-gray Stetson classic fedora with a burgundy and gold band matching the colors adorning King Cloud. Even in my own admittance, he looks sharp and dapper.

"How is King feeling tonight?" he asks with genuine concern, although it probably spawns as much from a desire to win as it does for any intimacy or care for the horse.

Dad responds that King Cloud is ready to go and on those words, and with the start of the event coming ever closer, we leave for the fairground's main ring.

We all walk in silence, as if soldiers deep in reflection. I have no idea what thoughts are running through the heads of Dad, Uncle JT or Dr. Bachtel, but I imagine it to be close to my own: nervous, excited, and focused.

King Cloud nears the ring with an ever-present arrogance. It is obvious he expects to do well and seems fully aware of the situation. During this weekend, I have learned a great deal about the mindset of horses. They are very temperamental and very proud creatures. In King Cloud's case, this is rightfully so. He has a great deal to be proud of and hopefully after this evening's event that will be even more so the case.

Nearing the main ring, my eyes catch sight first of the packed grandstand. Every seat is filled with audience members dressed in their Sunday best. Their collective whispers reverberate loudly from around the manufactured grandstand. As my eyes continue examining everything, I next see eight of the eleven other horses already here.

In addition to King Cloud of course, other familiar horses are

Pretty Boys' Earl Gray, Lucky Guy from King's qualifying Class, Sweet Mary, Uncle Bill's Kentucky Sunrise, and Bulgia's Shades of Blue. Within a few minutes, the other remaining horses have joined us.

At five minutes to eight, the event is about to begin. Dad gives Dr. Bachtel a leg-up onto King Cloud, hands him the whip and reminds Dr. Bachtel that he likely will not need to use the instrument. He then also adds, "And remember to loosen your hands a bit and keep your heels down in the stirrups. If you do all that, King will take care of the rest..."

Then, turning his head, he whispers inaudibly into King's ear, giving him what I assume to be some calming words of advice. King shakes his head up and down in response to Dad's familiar voice and soon thereafter, all the entrants begin to make their way to the ring.

Dad, Uncle JT and I take our familiar position opposite the main ring railing along with the other trainers when Dad points out Momma and Aunts Julie and Kat in the stands. They are sitting across the way and as I give them a wave, they see me and reciprocate my gesture.

Within moments the ringmaster, who is the same gentlemen from yesterday in a similar black suit and fedora hat, walks out into the center of the main ring. "Ladies and Gentlemen, welcome to Canfield Fairground's final event at our show this weekend. This five gait presentation features the finest amateur horses from across the country and is sure to please everyone."

The crowd claps feverishly, but yet in control as any group of such civilized onlookers would while the ringmaster introduces the twelve contestants. They are lined up in the order they arrived, so King Cloud is ninth in line as the parade of horses makes its first introductory trot around the ring.

The colors woven into the hair of each horse adds a pleasing ambiance to the event, reminiscent of similar Greek events three thousand years earlier. The speed and strength as exhibited by each of the horses is readily apparent, even to the untrained eye. I can instantly tell why this is the culminating event of the weekend, as the energy surrounding the ring is impossible to ignore.

After a couple of laps around the ring so the fans from all angles can get a good look, the ringmaster bellows the first string of commands to the horses.

Over the next few minutes, the horses all begin with the first of the five gaits, the walk. I center my vision on King Cloud for this section of the event. In this gait, he alternately supports the weight of him and Dr. Bachtel by three legs, and then two legs in the following sequence.

After going through the motions of the walk, the entire process is repeated from the start, but with left and right sides reversed. All while this is going on, King Cloud's head is bouncing back and forth to help keep his balance, much as humans do when outstretching their hands walking a tight rope.

When performed to perfection, the advancing rear hoof

touches the ground ahead of the place at which the previously advancing front hoof touched the ground. This makes for a noticeably smoother walk. As King performs this, he does it nearly to perfection, moving in a patterned, 1-2-3-4 beat.

After each horse has done the walk for a little over five minutes, the ringmaster tells them all to move on to the trot.

Wanting to enjoy all the horses, or at least as many as I can, my focus moves to Sweet Mary for this gait. In the trot, she moves her legs in unison in diagonal pairs, moving forward at the same time. In particular, Sweet Mary is engaged in what is called a park trot. In gaited show horses such as these, this trot is held in the highest regard. It is a showy, flashy trot with extreme elevation of the legs. From the standpoint of the balance of the horse, this is a very stable gait, and as such, the horse does not need to make any balancing motions with its head and neck if performed correctly. As I look on, I see Sweet Mary is doing just that and performing the gait to the highest standards.

After a few minutes of the trot, the ringmaster tells all the participants to move on to the canter. My concentration moves to Pretty Boy's Earl Gray for this gait. It seems his comfort level is high when atop the horse. He looks more at ease there, and full of concentration.

In this gait, Earl Gray's right rear leg impels himself forward. During this beat, he is supported only by that single leg while the remaining three legs are moving forward. On the next beat, he catches himself on the left rear and right front legs while the other hind leg is still shortly in contact with the ground. Then, on the third beat, he catches himself on the left front leg while the diagonal pair is shortly still in contact with the ground.

As I listen to the horses canter, I can hear the three stages of the movement as though a drum has been struck three times in succession. After a quick reprise, the same three-beat occurs once again.

The same five-minute time limit comes and goes, and once more the ringmaster commands the riders to switch to the fourth gate, which is the slow gait. My attention moves to Kentucky Sunrise and I watch as in this gait the horse follows the same general sequence of movement as King Cloud performed with such perfection in the walk, but with an alternate rhythm and collection of the movements.

While the horses are performing, Dad informs me that the slow gait was developed from the pace, a gait that normally is seen in harness racing. In the pace, both legs on the left side move together and then both legs on the right side move together. The speed of the two-beat pace is even faster than the trot. As he tells me, Kentucky Sunrise shows me, and as with all the horses looks spectacular in his delivery. While performing, he keeps the length of the stride long with only a slight gap between the foot-falls, resulting in a gait that is intermediate in speed between the walk and the pace, and very smooth.

After the horses all have had the allotted time to run through the slow gait, the ringmaster orders each participant to move on to the final gait, the rack. For this gait, I focus primarily on Shades of Blue.

While performing this gait, Shades of Blue's speed is increased close to that of the slow gait, but instead of being a two-beat gait like the trot and the slow gait, he performs it as a four-beat gait with equal intervals between each beat. The rack is difficult to sit through for the rider because between beats the body of the horse actually falls. Each time another diagonal pair of legs hits the ground; the rider is given a strong upward impulsion and meets the horse with some force on the way back down. Therefore, it is up to the rider in this gait, more so than in any other, to stay focused and in control. No rider wants to ruin a horse's chance of success and especially not in a championship round.

While watching, I take notice of a thick lather forming around the halter and bit. This is a familiar sight to anyone who has seen a horse practice or compete, and it spawns from a mixture of sweat, saliva, and skill. A horse that is working itself hard almost always creates this lather, so it is definitely a good sign.

As the horses all increase their steps and animated action, my concentration on the event is broken by Dad whispering out, "C'mon Doc. Loosen your hands…"

As Dr. Bachtel and King Cloud approach our area, Dad motions to him that his hands are too tight. It seems from the corner of his eye, Dr. Bachtel notices and eases his grip, becoming more relaxed.

After about twenty-five minutes in total, the ringmaster commands all the horses to make their way twice more around the ring and then head toward the grassy infield and move into a singular line.

As this happens, the progression of horses looks like a marching band lined up in preparation of a national performance.

After they are all lined up, the judges approach each horse individually, and make notations on their uniformed posture. Each rider tips their hat to the judges and after each horse has properly been examined for the similar quality features as in the three gait, the judges have each rider move his horse back three to five steps.

On that motion, it is Dad's signal to get ready in preparation of helping with the dismounting of the saddle. Within a minute, the trainers are on the field, helping their owners as the three judges write down additional notations.

After the conformation, where the judges examine the horse in its entirety, Dad resaddles King Cloud and helps give Doc Bachtel a leg-up back onto the horse.

The entire process takes awhile, as all twelve horses need to be thoroughly examined. After completion, the judges confer and make their decision, handing it to the ringmaster.

"Ladies and Gentlemen, let's hear it for these twelve horses. The judges surely had their work cut out for them."

The crowd releases a controlled cheer, appropriate for this

type of show. We all then listen as the ringmaster continues on, "And now for the results. In fifth place and winner of $200 is Gypsy Girl, ridden by Dr. D.J Martin of Cambridge farms located in Kansas City, Missouri."

The applause once again resumes as Gypsy Girl, a light tan mare moves forward collecting her fifth place prize, pink ribbon, and trophy. After Gypsy Girl gives a quick trot around the entire ring for the benefit of the crowd, the ringmaster continues on, "In fourth place and winner of $250 is Silver Arrow, ridden by Mr. Gunner McGavin of Pine Oak farms located in Georgetown, Kentucky."

As Gypsy Girl did, Sliver Arrow receives his prized white ribbon and circles the ring. Upon completing, the ringmaster moves on, "And now, for our top three horses of the evening. In third place and winner of $300 is King Cloud, ridden by Dr. David Bachtel of The Dells Farm located in North Canton, Ohio."

My heart jumps and for a moment, I question whether or not I heard the ringmaster correctly. After I realize I did, I join the rest of the crowd in their excitement. The success we've had this weekend has been capped by our third place finish. And although it is 'only' third place, to even finish in the top three or as it is said, 'play to place...' is still an accomplishment. As Dr. Bachtel approaches, his demeanor is joyous and both he and King Cloud look as if they are floating on air.

The top three winners each have the opportunity to travel

twice around the ring, and King Cloud prances proudly. As they pass by us, Uncle JT and I motion to Dr. Bachtel a congratulations.

As he then makes his way out of the ring, we run to meet him while the ringmaster continues, "In second place and winner of $400 is Lucky Guy, ridden by Mr. CC Turner of Founders Farms in North Plainfield, New Jersey."

I do not watch the ring for Lucky Guy's acceptance, but remember him in detail from the qualifying round as he was in King Cloud's class. We meet up with Dad and Dr. Bachtel over by the waiting area adjoining the ring.

"Way to go Doc," Uncle JT says in a congratulatory tone.

"Yeah, real great work in there," Dad adds with a youthful exuberance as both men pat both the horse and its rider.

Before Dr. Bachtel can reply, we all turn and listen to the ringmaster one final time.

"Ladies and Gentlemen. We have eight horses remaining, but only one can be our Grand Prize winner. Lets all give a big round of applause to the Canfield Fairground's Grand Prize winner of $500 in this five-gait event, Earl Gray, ridden by Mr. Pete Jones of Miller and Miller Farms."

The crowd erupts into one final, sustained cheer for Pretty Boy and as he receives his prize and trots around the ring, he soaks in their adulation. We are all proud of him and what he accomplished through his hard work.

Over the next twenty minutes, the owners and trainers all

congratulate each other on not only a job well done in the final round, but also the entire weekend. Pretty Boy approaches Dad and says, "Well Tom, looks like I finally beat ya…"

"You sure did," Dad replies with a handshake. "You and Earl Gray sure did look real fine out there."

"Thank you. King Cloud looked real good too. Surprised we beat him," Pretty Boy replies sincerely.

"Ahhh, no need for that. You earned it today Pete. Real good work out there…" As they finish their conversation, Dr. and Mrs. Bachtel and Charles Miller, the owners of King Cloud and Earl Gray respectively approach Dad and Pretty Boy.

"Goodness Tom," Dr. Bachtel says happily, "We did great out here this weekend. A first place and a third place given the type of competition here this weekend is fantastic."

"I agree with David," Mrs. Bachtel says. Then with a smile she adds, "Good job Thomas."

"You and Doc did real well ridden' those horses Mrs. B. It makes my job easy."

"Either way. Good work," Dr. Bachtel says as he pats Dad on the shoulder. "Now I have to go meet up with the owners, we are going to have ourselves a little party tonight."

"Funny, so are us trainer folk. Should be a good time."

"Well deserved too Tom. Now take care of these horses and we'll get together later this week.

After the congratulations are all done, the horsemen quickly disperse as the horses all still need to cool down. No one wants to injure the horse because of being a little over-excited.

On our way back to the stable, I overhear Uncle JT ask Dad, "So Mojo. You think you could'a pushed King to first over Pretty Boy if you were riding him?"

"Tough to say. Doc was a little tight, but Pete rode that horse of his real good. Tough to say."

"I think you could've. That's for sure."

"I appreciate the kind words, really I do. Either way though, I sure am glad it worked out as it did. Third place...."

"And first in the three," I add in from beside the two men.

"That's right. And first in the three gait. That's one hell of a weekend. One hell of a weekend."

Then, after a slight pause as we all reflect on Dad's words, Uncle JT whispers, "Amen..."

Chapter 19

Later in the evening, about an hour after the show which gave us plenty of time to finish the cooling down period for King Cloud and the bedding of the rest of the horses, it is finally time for some relaxation. The entire group of horsemen and their families are all getting together for dinner and dancing, and it is an event everyone is looking forward to.

During the competition, some of the wives, girlfriends and children of the horsemen would show up on the final day of the event for the party, a tradition started long ago. The party takes place at the fairgrounds, right around the tack area. Although limited finances is certainly a key reason for the fairground location for our party, another paramount factor is many of the hotels would not accept Blacks as tenants.

The women hand make picnic baskets of food filled with chicken, ham, greens, corn bread, potato salad, jam cake, and peach cobbler. In the case of Aunt Julie, her food is talked about all over North Middletown, Kentucky and I assume all over the many fairgrounds she visited when Uncle Frank showed horses. In fact years later, the wealthy Kentuckian farm she was hired as a cook encouraged and supported the printing of a cookbook filled with Aunt Julie's recipes. Unfortunately, only the initial draft of that book's top few recipes was printed before her untimely death.

While we were working hard all weekend, Momma, Aunt Kat and Aunt Julie were back home preparing and cooking the food we would all be enjoying tonight, and we are all looking forward to a little bit of home cookin'.

The party starts late this evening, about ten in the evening, and everyone is sitting around eating and drinking. For the horsemen and the women, the drink of choice for this special occasion is Old Fitzgerald Kentucky bourbon. For me and the other kids, we stick to pop, but drink it without restraint from our parents. Plenty of pop is a pure joy.

As guessed, the conversation centers primarily on the weekend and all of our successes. Several of these horsemen had a least one horse from their farm make it to the final round, with Pretty Boy taking top honors.

"So, how's it feel?" Uncle Bill asks out to Pretty Boy.

"How's what feel?" he replies, taking a swig of bourbon.

"Your success! You pretty much beat us all."

"That's nice for sure," Pretty Boy says. "But beating those white folks was even better."

"I bet they ain't celebrating their night with no chocolate chips," Bulgia interjects in reference to his familiar tagline.

"Ain't that for sure," Uncle JT adds with a raised glass as everyone else toasts in accompaniment.

I found out during this evening while everyone was discussing the results of the show, that the Lemon Drop Kid did end up taking first place in the Fine Harness. Of the three events, that was the only horse who won first place that was not part of this fraternity, which in itself is a testament to the talent of all these men.

The joyful gathering is filled with laughter and fun, led mostly by the antics of Uncle JT and Pretty Boy. Both men love the spotlight, but the former yearns for it in a less desirable tone. Nevertheless, once a few drinks were in the both of them... and the rest of the group for that matter, the party really starts to get going.

From my vantage point it is fun to watch. Devouring my second plate of food, I watch in earnest the entertainment before me. In this weekend, I have learned a great deal about the horsemen and feel as much a part of their group as any of them, mainly because of their own admittance of me into their fraternity with open arms.

Uncle JT, having had a little too much Kentucky bourbon, prepares to eat a sandwich and while talking reaches for what he thinks is the ketchup bottle when in fact it is the hot sauce bottle. We all notice this as he pours and pours on more ketchup, or at least in his hazy state he thinks its ketchup. We all watch with silent mirth building within us.

I try to warn him, but before I can get out my words Dad puts his hand over my mouth. Then in my stead he says, "Hey Country Boy. Why don't you have yourself another sip of that fine Kentucky bourbon?"

"To Kentucky," Uncle JT says as he raises his glass. "Home

to the finest horses and the finest bourbon…"

The group collectively raises their drinks together to his words, toasting their good lives and the good fortune of the weekend. After kicking back a swig of the potent alcohol, Uncle JT takes a big bite of his sandwich. Instantly, as the hot sauce ravages his taste buds, his eyes light up and he quickly reaches for a glass of water. Knowing this was going to happen, Momma already had a glass of water ready and handed it to him.

We all laugh, not at him, but with him. Ok, maybe we did laugh at him, but he joined in with us.

After the incident, Dad moves closer to Uncle JT and I can hear him talk about his chance to finally dance with Aunt Kat. I know that Uncle JT has always been very shy around her, but his love for her is genuine.

"You gonna ask Kat to dance? She's been waitin' patiently all night."

"I can't do it Mojo. I just ain't got it in me," he whispers to my dad quietly so few others could hear him.

In response, Dad reminds him of the practice in the barn they had with the pitchfork… even as recently as a couple nights ago. "Just remember," Dad adds, "Hold her gently, and listen to the music as you feel her close to your heart."

Uncle JT kicks back two shots of the bourbon and replies, "Alright Mojo. I'm ready…"

In aid of his friend, Dad moves over to the hi-fi and puts on Sam Cooke, specifically *I Love You For Sentimental Reasons*.

He chose the selection because just as it calmed the horses, it had the same affect on the men... especially Uncle JT. Having spent so much time listening to Sam Cooke in such calm and familiar situations, it is the perfect choice.

As Dad goes over to dance with Momma, Uncle JT shyly approaches Aunt Kat and asks her to dance. She accepts with a warm smile, looking like she wondered what took so long. As they are dancing, Dad looks at Uncle JT over Momma's shoulder and smiles while lip-synching the words to the song in Momma's ear, "*I love you for sentimental reasons...*"

Seeing this, Uncle JT leans in and softly sings the next verse of the song in Aunt Kat's ear.

This continues on, with neither woman knowing they are connected by the suave ploys of a pilot and his loyal wingman.

Well past midnight, my eyes are droopy and the party is starting to wind down. Tomorrow morning everyone will be picking up their stables and will not see each other until the next show. It is a somber time, with that emotion probably heightened by the bourbon.

It would be the last time I ever saw all these men together and the only time I would have the opportunity to witness this fraternity first hand. The following summer and summers beyond, I became actively involved in organized sports that kept me away from the summer horse shows. Dad encouraged me to play baseball during the summers, intentionally to keep me away from the horse training business.

Five years later Dad was hospitalized with lung cancer and had his left lung removed from all the years of smoking unfiltered Camel cigarettes. After his hospitalization and unable to continue working with the horses, we moved off the farm to the city life in Canton, Ohio, where he died a year later riding a horse in a Alzheimer's dream state.

In the years to follow, some of the Mighty Middletown Horsemen did eventually ride horses in shows, but still, each of them would be forgotten. Not Pretty Boy, not Bulgia, not Uncle Bill or Uncle JT, nor my father... not one of them remembered beyond their own blood, their own lineage... the contribution they had on the American Saddlebred Horse world. Their role in the progression of training horses is second only to that of Tom Bass'. However, while Tom Bass is barely known, the rest of these horsemen have all but been forgotten, lost underneath a blanket of culture which gave such little significance to people of color.

These horsemen impacted and changed my life, each other's lives and Saddlebred horse riding. Yet, except for a few pictures handed down from father to child, and then again from child to their own progeny, and now long since locked away in a forgotten attic, there is very little which links their efforts to their deeds. Deeds which have shaped history.

Epilogue

1976

Kean College

Union Township, New Jersey

My senses are jarred back to the present by the first student coming forward with a finished test paper in hand. Looking up at the clock, I see there is only a minute left and I address the class accordingly. After a few final scribbles on their papers, I notify them all to put their pencils down. The class stands and starts to bring up their papers, one by one as they leave the classroom.

While they are doing this, I try to keep bottled within the emotion that is strong inside of me. I could not have imagined a better way to spend the passing time than thinking of that weekend in 1959.

It takes only a few minutes for the classroom to clear out entirely. Without delaying, I organize all the papers and place them within my briefcase as I then also exit the classroom.

As I walk down the hall to my office, I see several students pass. Then suddenly I take notice of a student walking toward me while looking down at an icy tray of water she had just filled and is now retuning to our department's community refrigerator. While she is slowly and carefully walking, looking down at the tray in deep concentration, water continuously spills over with each step.

As we are about to pass each other, I stop her and tell her my dad once taught me that if you do not look down at the water it won't spill. The student looks at me with bewilderment and replies, "Really?"

"Try it," I respond smiling.

She takes a step forward, and then another. She walks very slowly for the next five yards looking straight ahead without spilling any water and as she turns right into the department's kitchen, she turns and looks at me with a mystifying smile and says, "Thanks Mr. Downing!"

I give her a wave and with Dad still on my mind I head toward our department's office. As I walk in, a few of my colleagues are in conversation and welcome me warmly.

"So what are you doing this weekend Lee," my mentor and friend Dr. Darden asks me.

"Well," I reply. "I think I'm going to go through some old photos and some old memories."

"That is always fun," our secretary Celia replies. "What are you planning on remembering?"

"My dad..."

"I miss my father," Celia continues. "What did your father do?"

"He was a horse trainer."

"Really? We have friends that ride horses," adds our chair

of the department, Dr. Benson. "They love their horses. Was your dad any good at it?"

"One of the best," I reply as I finish packing my materials for the weekend. "He was part of the Bourbon County Horsemen, or as I called them, The Mighty Middletown Horsemen."

"Never heard of them unfortunately," Dr. Benson replies with a shocked look to my answer.

Then, as I am walking out the door I finish off softly, "No one has... that's the problem. No one has..."

Final Thoughts

Although many years have passed since that memorable weekend with my dad and his fellow horsemen, I still find myself recalling those days. That is especially true whenever I see a horse trailer traveling down the interstate or when watching horses graze on green grass as I pass by in my car. Each time, I smile and think how blessed I have been to experience such a moment in life.

There is an old adage I once heard, "Memory is the only way home." As I think back to that memorable weekend in 1959, going home makes me proud and content. In my comfortable lifestyle, I often wonder in amazement how my dad and his fellow horsemen managed to persevere through those times, all the while still finding ways to ensure my smooth journey through life.

The great Jackie Robinson once said, "A life is not important except in the impact it has on other lives." My dad and the forgotten horsemen certainly had an impact, not only on my life but on the lives of many. Their impact was made without substantial amounts of money or materialistic items, but with their teachings of courage, respect and dignity. All virtues, unlike money or materialism, which last a lifetime.

Printed in the United States
107005LV00005B/7-15/A

9 781599 758800